# Almost Nothing To Be Scared Of

WISCONSIN POETRY SERIES
Ronald Wallace, Series Editor

# Almost Nothing To Be Scared Of

## David Clewell

THE UNIVERSITY OF WISCONSIN PRESS

The University of Wisconsin Press
1930 Monroe Street, 3rd Floor
Madison, Wisconsin 53711-2059
uwpress.wisc.edu

3 Henrietta Street, Covent Garden
London WC2E 8LU, United Kingdom
eurospanbookstore.com

Printed in the United States of America
This book may be available in a digital edition.

Library of Congress Cataloging-in-Publication Data
Names: Clewell, David, 1955– author.
Title: Almost nothing to be scared of / David Clewell.
Other titles: Wisconsin poetry series.
Description: Madison, Wisconsin : The University of Wisconsin Press,
[2016] | ©2016 | Series: Wisconsin poetry series
Identifiers: LCCN 2015036811 | ISBN 9780299307240 (pbk. ; alk. paper)
Classification: LCC PS3553.L42 A6 2016 | DDC 811/.54—dc23 LC
record available at http://lccn.loc.gov/2015036811

Book design: Alcorn Publication Design

*for Patricia and Ben—*

*Superman had his Fortress of Solitude,*
*but I much prefer the two of you—*
*my Sources of Fortitude . . .*

# ❈ CONTENTS ❧

## II. Civility Was All the Rage

## III. Interlude: A Dozen from the Dream Chair

## IV. As Long As We Keep Going

## V. Epilogue

# ❖ ACKNOWLEDGMENTS ❖

Grateful acknowledgment is made to the editors of the following publications where many of these poems first appeared:

*Boulevard*: "Despite What You Might Have Heard to the Contrary, the Hand Is Never Quicker Than the Eye"

*Brilliant Corners*: "My One-Performance-Only Dream: Night of the Jazz Giants' Shoes"; "Trying on Hats with Rahsaan Roland Kirk"

*December*: "Since So Many People Don't Seem to Know What *No Soliciting* Means, I Tried to Spell It Out More Fully on My Front Door"

*The Georgia Review*: "At the Convention of State Librarians, I Should Have Been Preaching to the Choir"; "*Do Not Overinflate*"; "In 1966 Debbie Fuller Was Sweet on Pluto"

*MARGIE/American Journal of Poetry*: "Too Far This Time"

*Natural Bridge*: "Here's to the Moon: Goodbye" (Section ii—"My Uncle's Dilemma")

*New Letters*: "The Bartender Doesn't Ask Much" (Section i); "If We Were to Experience an Outbreak Like That One in Ancient Thrace"; "The Real Story of Adam and Eve, Wherein the True Cradle of Civilization Is Revealed"; "Sonata for Tornado in EF-5 (Major): May 22, 2011, 5:41–6:13 p.m."; "There Was a Time We Weren't Afraid of Saying *That Is All*"

*New Ohio Review*: "Quality Control"

*Plume*: "Acknowledgments: This Poem Would Not Have Been Possible"; "Between the '60s and the Saucers and the Willy-Nilly Gods—Let Alone the Vagaries of Ordinary Mortals—It's Hard to Know Who Needs Believing Most"; "Cryptozoology 101: The Academics Have a Point, and Yet Once Again They Miss a Much Larger One"

*Profane*: "Charlie the Tuna: A Matter of Taste"; "The Doctor's Wife"; "Last-Ditch Prayer for the Lovers"

*River Styx*: "A Lesson from My Brief History in Professional Wrestling"; "Tonight's Feature: *Revenge of the Inside-Out, Multiple-Personalities Haiku*"

*UCity Review*: "The Bartender Doesn't Ask Much" (Section ii, as "*I Could Care Less*, Said the Bartender"); "Why Plans 1 through 8 from Outer Space Came Undone—and Plan 9, Too, for That Matter"

"Because It Was the Year the Mayan Calendar Ran Out, Some People Feared the Worst in 2012" (Section i) appeared as part of *The World Keeps Turning to Light: A Renga by the State Poets Laureate of America*, edited by Caryn Mirriam-Goldberg (Negative Capability).

"*Greetings from Roswell, New Mexico: Home of the Historic 1947 Flying Saucer Crash*" was published, in an earlier version, as part of *The Conspiracy Quartet* (Garlic Press).

"Man Ray Stares into the Future of Jazz" was included in *Heart to Heart: New Poems Inspired by Twentieth-Century American Art*, edited by Jan Greenberg (Abrams).

"What If All Along We've Been Wrong About Tinfoil Hats" was included in *Privacy Policy: The Anthology of Surveillance Poetics*, edited by Andrew Ridker (Black Ocean).

In addition to the aforementioned editors, a few assiduous, trustworthy readers looked at many of these poems in earlier incarnations; my thanks to Murray Farish, Cat-Man Harrison, Slats Lattimore, and Dale Woolery—as well as to my beloved dedicatees, who also on a nearly daily basis put up with both my gibber and my jabber.

I'm beholden to the Dream Chair: my gratitude for Section IV.

Thanks to David Wilson, former dean of Webster University's College of Arts & Sciences, for his generous support of the eccentric research that underpins some of these poems.

A heap of gratitude to Patricia (yes, *again!*), whose dogged international sleuthing tracked down the provenance of what's become my flat-out-favorite Cold War–era photograph—and to Peer-Olaf Richter in Hamburg, Germany, who so graciously facilitated its appropriation here. I'm hoping that, sometimes, you *can* judge a book by its cover.

Hats off to the good folks at the University of Wisconsin Press who worked with me, probably because they drew the short straws: Amber, Sheila, and Carla. Hats way off to Adam Mehring, project editor extraordinaire—who's no doubt glad that at least this time around, in the name of fact-checking, he didn't have to watch and rewatch footage of a frustrated Buzz Aldrin throwing his wild punch on a Los Angeles sidewalk. Compared to that, spending time with a hyphenated-or-not yellow polka dot bikini is surely an itsy bitsy matter.

And special thanks, long overdue, to Ron Wallace for more than forty years (*yikes!*) of good counsel, support, and camaraderie.

*How'd you like to gaze at a beer can throughout eternity?*
*It might not be so bad. There'd be nothing to fear.*
        —Philip K. Dick, *A Scanner Darkly*


*Take off your pants, he said.*
*He had an egg in his hand.*

*Anything for the angel of death.*
        —Frank Stanford, "The Angel of Death"

# Almost Nothing To Be Scared Of

## Quality Control

This poem was inspected by Number 99
and found free of the usual, obvious defects:
dropped stitches, misaligned seams, or loose threads.
And considering the working conditions of the world,
where it's amazing these things ever get done at all,
I think it turned out better than anyone expected.

I hope this poem is some small comfort to you
right up until the day you'll no longer recall it—
not even its name or the tiniest trace of whatever
once so delighted you here. There is no lifetime
guarantee. That would be counterproductive on our part,
really—we who just can't seem to quit making new ones.

# Acknowledgments: This Poem Would Not Have Been Possible

without my friends and colleagues who read earlier versions, knowing
anything they might have thought of suggesting would have fallen
on the same deaf ears that strung this thing together in the first place;

without every one of those teachers who encouraged me wholeheartedly
to take up metallurgy or, better yet, some kind of self-defense or
maybe one of those hopeless ball-toss operations in a traveling carnival;

without the dozens of venture capitalists who hazarded their guesses—
there wouldn't be nearly enough return in any of this dubious business—
and so decided not to venture even in my general direction;

without Walt Whitman, who wanted more poets, singers, and orators
but obviously didn't foresee just how long it might take me
to scrape my boot-soles pretty near clean of all that gab and loitering;

without Thomas Pynchon, Don DeLillo, and Roger Patterson's Bigfoot,
who asked no fatuous questions in never-ending Q&A sessions,
nor did they otherwise go out of their way to embarrass me in public;

without everyone I'm forgetting at the moment, to whom
I'd like to say *Hey, you know who you are*, except I'm not at all certain
that any of us can ever really know who we are—so forget it;

without these very words that somehow worked things out once more
among themselves instead of just throwing up their tiny pica hands
when I went missing for hours or whole days and nights at a time;

without my alien abductors, who almost always put me back
exactly where they'd found me—at the open Frigidaire,

4

behind the humming typewriter, or sleeping in my not-so-easy chair;

without the discerning editor whose unmistakably sophisticated taste
led to this publication—and since your good name's already on the line,
why not make that literal and write yourself in here, although it spells
the end of these tidy three-line stanzas: _____;

without my sharp-eyed son who will report it stolen straightaway if
this turns up somewhere I'd never willingly submit to; any publication,
rebroadcast, or other transmission of this poem—without the express
written consent of the author or Major League Poetry—is prohibited;

without those keeping track of their frequent-reader pages, who must now
return all seat-backs and tray-tables to the upright and locked position;
we were hardly airborne and already we're descending, but rest assured
there's no way I could have imagined even this scant flight of fancy

without every last one of you.

# I.

# Someone's Gone and Done It Now

○ ○ ○ ○ ○ ○ ○ ○ ○

*Well most things that I know, I didn't learn in class.*
*The road don't go forever, so ride it while it lasts.*
*If you're gonna raise a ruckus, one word of advice:*
*If you're gonna do wrong, buddy, do wrong right.*

—The Devil Makes Three, *Do Wrong Right*

## The Real Story of Adam and Eve, Wherein the True Cradle of Civilization Is Revealed

And it so happened they were driven out of Eden
in God's fire-red Pontiac convertible—a sensible car, really,
for an almighty God who wasn't above giving them a lift.
When they reached the edge of the continent, the end of the road
such as it was, God let them out, there on the Jersey shore.
Then He turned around, burning serious rubber,
and peeled out straightaway for the Catskills or the Poconos
or whatsoever used to pass for Paradise here on Earth.

It was just the two of them for what surely had to seem
like an eternity. This was the Jersey shore, after all, before
picture postcards or saltwater taffy, before suntan oil,
beach umbrellas, or T-shirt emporiums. Before the Stone Pony
where, I'm sorry, not every fan making the claim
truly could have heard a young Springsteen back in the day.
Even before Skee-Ball or that one annoying guy always
way too good at guessing your weight every summer.

The sign said NO SWIMMING AFTER DARK, so
they didn't—having grown considerably more circumspect
since the last time they went against the wishes of Management.
Still, they figured it might be all right to go naked
once more and not be ashamed. Those were days of good cheer
in the Garden, but this time Adam couldn't stop humming
*Itsy Bitsy Teeny Weeny Yellow Polka Dot Bikini*. Even though
the words were impossibly beyond him, Eve in a bikini was not.

Adam decided he had to keep busy and, accordingly, each morning
he went to work. By the sweat of his brow, and plank by plank,
he built a boardwalk that went on famously for miles.
Immediately Eve set up shop as a psychic—*Madame Eve*—
with the speal-bone of a ram she'd lifted from God's glove box
and some coins she'd managed to fish out of the sand
with the metal detector that God in His infinite wisdom
had tossed out of His car right before making His getaway.

Then Adam spent his days naming the carnival rides that Eve saw
whirring away in the future. He couldn't wait for the Tilt-A-Whirl.
He took up smoking and practiced the surly demeanor of the first-ever
ride operator. The devil was in the details, of course—they'd both need
paying customers, and this was as fine a reason as any
to spend their nights by the fire, buoyed by the pounding waves:
they would be fruitful, multiplying the sweet hell out of each other
until once more the world was teeming, and they were the ones
this time who saw, lo and behold, that it was good.

## Despite What You Might Have Heard to the Contrary, the Hand Is Never Quicker Than the Eye

*No matter how confident you are in your dexterity and patter, always refuse (as politely as possible) any request to* do it again. *Given a second chance, someone might be able to see this time how you've "done it," spoiling the illusion.*
> —from instructions included with "The Dancing Handkerchief" (1935)

—which is amazing, given the elaborate mechanics of the eye and everything
the light goes through before it makes any sense: the cornea, the aqueous
humour, the pupil, the lens, the vitreous humour, until it's dispensed among
the retina's dizzying one hundred twenty-six million rods and cones
producing chemicals that create each electrical impulse to be transmitted
through the optic nerve to the primary visual cortex somewhere
way in the back of the brain, where whatever you've just been looking at
for better or for worse or for absolutely no good reason at all finally
takes recognizable shape. This transpires in nanoseconds, in the blink
of, well . . . an eye, before your hand can lift a cup of coffee even
halfway up to your impatient lips.

Any sleight of hand depends
on careful misdirection, inducing the eye at just the right moment
to focus on the wrong thing entirely. Take that girl sprawled out tonight
in the Chevrolet's back seat. She always picks up right away on anything
her boyfriend's trying to pull off. He's usually all awkward hands,
but this time it's going down another way instead: somehow
he's managed to whisper a few practiced words in her ear, and
that's caused her just now to look into the future she's thinking could be

theirs together, and by the time she's back, eyes wide open then
and there in the Chevy-back-seat moment, she's in no position to insist
she never saw this coming. She doesn't quite know how he did it
or how she did it either, really, when all is said and mostly done.
And surely no one would be terribly surprised to hear
each of them asking the other to do whatever that exactly was again.

# A Lesson from My Brief History in Professional Wrestling

## i.

When I was in The Show, I was one of the mostly Good Guys who,
like good guys everywhere, was bound sometimes to go off-script,
flying off the top rope and coming down a little too hard
on some Bad Guy I'd just finished laying low. And then behind
the referee's back, I'd rather theatrically make ready to unleash
whatever extravagant move that a given night's drama called for
while my opponent, instantly contrite but no less fundamentally
evil, would drag himself to his knees and plead for mercy,
shaking his head full of exaggerated worry. And whenever
something like that happens, I'm here to tell you: Do not
hesitate. Don't leave yourself open to the cartoon sucker-punch.

That's the moment it always dawns on someone in the crowd,
some loudmouthed master-of-the-obvious who thinks maybe
he's the first person ever to get to the bottom of over
100 years of this whole pro wrestling situation: *It isn't real.*
Do tell, Mr. Ringside Einstein. If he writes up that kind of insight,
he's liable to land a job in yet another university's Popular—
don't ever say *Pop*—Culture Studies program where they study
the fun right out of everything that clearly should have been.

## ii.

I'm betting you could use a few unlikely moves yourself
in the world we actually live in. Wouldn't you love to know every
once in a while, even before your day begins, precisely

how it's going to turn out? With no one like a referee in sight,
you could take down the disagreeable clerk at the DMV
with The Flying Clothesline or The Inverted Atomic Drop.
For the supercilious waiter, I'd recommend The Gator Buster
or The Crossface Chickenwing. The Frankenstein Avalanche
or The Sleeper will put the kibosh on that couple's nonstop talking
at the movies. Save The Jumping Piledriver or The Hammer-Bomb
for the *We're-already-working-in-your-neighborhood* salesman,
and for the next Jehovah's Witness at the door, it's time
for The Tree of Woe or else the bewildering Lady of the Lake.

Yeah, they might end up nursing their small share of pain tonight,
never quite knowing what hit them, but come tomorrow
they'll be back at their familiar stations, none the worse
for mortal wear. And if you wake up imagining that,
from now on, things surely will be different, that everyone involved
has learned at last some valuable lesson, then sadly—
aside from a handful of moves that sounded way too good to be true—
a century of pro wrestling really hasn't taught you much of anything.

## There Was a Time We Weren't Afraid of Saying *That Is All*

*Thomas Edison is credited with instigating the practice of saying* Hello *when answering the telephone—and for the word's subsequent popularity as a greeting. His inventor-rival Alexander Graham Bell preferred* Ahoy *and answered the phone that way for the rest of his life.*
   —Ammon Shea, The Phone Book

### i.

Before the telephone, *Hello* was used
to get someone's attention fast: *Hello,*
*what do you think you're doing? Cats weren't meant*
*to fly, so put her down.* Or to express
a form of mild surprise: *Hello, what have*
*we here? A flying cat? Hello? Hello.*

Despite Bell's stubborn preference for *Ahoy,*
the world's first published phonebook said *Hello*
would be a good idea when picking up
to let the caller know you're on the line.
It warned against *improper language* that
*should be reported posthaste to this office.*

While people got acquainted with the notion
of talking to someone they couldn't see,
they tried out lines that didn't quite catch on
like *Are you really there?* and *Did I get you?*
But not so much *Ahoy*, which seemed too nautical
a greeting to extend across dry land.

The phonebook recommended *That is all*
when you'd said everything you had to say

and *God be with you* might be overreaching,
but He sneaked in and never left, disguised
as something far less spiritually bracing—
*Goodbye*. And someone's gone and done it now.

Police departments loved the ring of *That
is all*—the perfect two-way-radio sign-off.
Another day's pursuit would then begin
and one more citizen, ready or not,
could kiss his sorry, law-abiding (*please
report improper language*) ass goodbye.


## ii.

And here's the part where I say *That is all*
should be resuscitated in our time,
a useful and straightforward declaration—
*there's nothing more to say or do. I'm done*:

tonight a soldier's heartbeat has gone AWOL,
one lover's walking out another's door,
the gunman's gone as far as *Ready, aim*,
the waitress quits mid-shift before she's fired,
the stripper's down to nothing left to lose,
the carnival's in town but it's not open,
the Human Cannonball's not coming down,
the factory worker turns off her machine,
the baby finally quiets into dreaming,
and in his breathless encore Sonny Rollins
now blows away the crowd with one long note
he won't call back into his horn until
he's out of sight offstage—and even then
he might decide this isn't over yet.

### iii.

There's heavy lifting going on tonight
and maybe, for a change, that won't be all
for nothing. Let's say someone's load is lightened,
that Porky Pig took elocution lessons:
his *That's all, folks!* goes off without a hitch.
And Keats' *beauty-truth-truth-beauty* bit
sounds good, but is that really all we know
on Earth? We need to know. And living out
our days between *Hello* and *That is all*,
we hope the *next time* in our *Better-luck-
next-time* is headed our way fairly soon.

If what arrives is less than we expected,
too small to change our lives all by itself,
then how about providing us at least
a place to catch our breath? That's pretty much
what good poems—never mind a thing like this
*Hello-what-have-we-here* affair of mine—
on their best days are more than glad to offer.
They make their stand in the thick of the world
to reinvent what's possible again,
and never once do they just phone it in.

Ahoy, hello, or do you read me? *Over
and out* is so much easier to say
than do. Than to be done with. Done for good.
At times we'll say something's as good as done,
but in real life it hardly ever is.
We mean to say it actually will happen—
and quickly too, if we have anything
to say about it. Or to say at all.

I know I have a lot of *say* in these
last lines, so please forgive me. I don't mean
to waste my breath or yours when nothing is
as good as done that isn't done already.

## When I Called the National Security Agency to Complain About the Indiscriminate Collection of Private Citizens' Telephone Records, I Was Put on *Hold* for a Suspiciously Long Time

*Your call is very important to us. All your calls, as you must know,*
*are very important to us. This particular call may be monitored*
*for quality-control purposes or for no good reason we can think of.*
*Just because we can. Because these days, you never know.*
*Please remain on the line until we've made a proper threat*
*assessment. Calls will be answered strictly in order of priority.*
*If you've got nothing to hide, you've got absolutely nothing*

*to fear. This is still America last time we checked,*
*and we're doing everything in our power to keep it that way.*
*No one's ever guilty of anything as long as they can prove otherwise,*
*so please remain on the line. This country's storied history is one*
*of human ingenuity: we've always made it up as we go along.*
*Right now we're flying by the seat of our Patriot-Act balloon-pants,*
*but hey, at least we're still here, and we're especially glad*
*that you're part of this too, so please remain on the line.*

*That your Walgreens prescriptions have been ready for days*
*is not a threat, although they might reduce your mounting anxiety.*
*That you haven't spoken to your mother in weeks doesn't much*
*concern us either, but you don't want to hear the trash she's talking.*
*And frankly, we didn't realize anyone was still giving money to*
*Greenpeace. We're long past caring about that—go save the whales,*
*but you could have sprung for much better seats down at the stadium.*

*Please remain on the line. Due to the extraordinarily high volume*
*of calls nationwide, your estimated wait time would be*
*just a wilder, more worthless guess than usual on our part. Someone*
*surely will be with you, though, sooner or later. So listen carefully*
*for a voice on the line or a knock on the door or even someone*
*bumping into the rearranged furniture in your dark living room.*
*And that's no lie, nor is it a threat. Consider it a promise, made*
*right here in America, where* Security *is our middle name,*
*and right now you need to remain on the line more than ever before.*

*The only thing we can never know for certain is tomorrow's weather.*
*There's no percentage in it for us, anyway—there's no stopping it*
*before it happens, ever. That's how weather is. It isn't ricin or*
*anthrax or fertilizer bombs. You can gather all the best intelligence*
*in the world, but if it rains, you're still going to get wet.*
*So please remain on the line, where it's always nice and dry.*

*We know where you live. We know how you live. It's almost as if,*
*oddly enough, you're a friend, but still we have no idea why*
*some outmoded notion of privacy is so damn important to you,*
*someone with nothing to hide. Nothing to be afraid of.*
*That's the reason every one of your calls is so very important to us.*
*If you want to be a dog with a bone, then you can count on us to be*
*the bigger, many-headed dog you'll never piss with, and rest assured*
*we've got a few bones of our own that we're not about to let go of.*

*Please remain on the line, even though we know already, word*
*for indignant, self-righteous word, what you're going to say,*
*and all because last night you felt strangely compelled to run it by*
*your old college professor of creative writing, who couldn't imagine*
*anything so important that you had to call him at 2 in the morning,*
*especially when, truth be told, it wasn't really much of a poem*
*he ended up only pretending to listen to, anyway.*

## Since So Many People Don't Seem to Know What *No Soliciting* Means, I Tried to Spell It Out More Fully on My Front Door

*Here there will be no Saving-the-Whales. No Feeding-the-Children.*
*No Girl Scout Cookies. No Organic Milk Home Delivery.*
*No Running-for-Office-and-I-Need-Your-Vote.*
*No Walking-for-the-Cure-and-I-Need-More-Sponsors.*
*No Alien-Greys-from-Andromeda-Down-on-Their-Gas-Money-Luck.*
*No Working-My-Way-Through-School-by-Bothering-You.*
*No Do-You-Need-Firewood? No Do-You-Have-Canned-Goods?*
*No Home Improvers. No Gutters of Gutters.*
*No Pour-You-a-Driveway, Mow-Your-Lawn, or Shovel-Your-Snow?*
*Nothing* Watchtower-*titled.* (Unless you're Dylan or Hendrix.)
*No Help-Send-My-High-School-Band-to-Brazil.* (And I suppose
you'll be coming back?) *No Have-Any-Odd-Jobs?* (Not at the moment,
but I worked three seasons guessing weights on the carnival midway.)
*No Could-You-Use-a-Home-Security-System?* (Sure, *now*
you ask me. Where were you about fifteen lines earlier?)

Nor was I expecting the woman at my door who informed me
that I forgot to list *No Prostitutes*—clearly the very first thing
*No Soliciting* made her think of. I said I'd never really thought of them
as the door-to-door type, exactly, let alone even a little bit annoying.
But surely she wasn't by some chance a prostitute herself, thereby
proving me wrong on both counts, was she?

*O Sweet Jesus, no,*
*although in college, yes, I did flirt briefly with Theater. But anyway,*

she was simply walking her dog and thought I might like to know that
a couple of Jehovah's Witnesses and one real-pissed-off Girl Scout
were letting the air out of my tires and jamming a box of Thin Mints,
one cookie at a time, into the gas tank.

                                        And when I sighed and said
I guess I'll phone AAA, she took my hand and called me brave, *so brave*
for owning up, just like that, to my rather obvious drinking problem—
likely the source of my negative thinking and actively antisocial behavior
posted right there on the door, *Sweet Jesus*, for everyone to see.

## The Guy on the Corner Is Snapping His Fingers to Keep the Elephant Jokes Away

### i.

A preacher, a nun, and a rabbi go into a bar.
Everyone in the place knows
this is some kind of joke
they've been part of many times before,
except for the blonde who's just walked in
and immediately doesn't get it.

### ii.

A preacher, a nun, and a rabbi go into a conference room
where they discuss the tenets and traditions of their faiths
and manage to come to a deeper understanding
of their shared humanity—or else they're in there
cracking themselves up with knock-knock jokes
where the answer's always *God*.

### iii.

A preacher, a nun, and a rabbi go into a coma,
and this could quite possibly mean the end
of humor as we've come to know it in our time.
But they might have the last laugh yet,
their heavenly reward: all the chicken
they can eat when they get to the Other Side.

## Charlie the Tuna: A Matter of Taste

**i.**

Always Charlie *the* Tuna, if you please. Never just plain
Charlie Tuna. He's no ordinary member of the Tuna family.
He's not just one of the fishy hoi polloi. Like God and his *I am*
*that I am* from inside the burning bush—when Moses asked
with whom did he have the pleasure of speaking, so that he might
tell his people where the hell he'd been, what had taken so long—
Charlie the Tuna undeniably is that he is, too,
but without the heavy-handed drama of shrubbery on fire.
It would have been so much easier for Moses if he could have
simply told his people that Charlie sent him.

**ii.**

Created in advertising's animated image of a beatnik, 1961,
Charlie sported dark glasses and something like a beret until
that craze, like, finally faded. Then his glasses lightened up,
became semi-studious horn-rims. Artist Tom Rogers drew Charlie
based on an unlikely friend who played a little jazz in the Village,
but Charlie's offbeat voice was straight out of Brooklyn—
a prescient bit of hipster typecasting decades ahead of its time.

**iii.**

And no insipid tuna-fish jingle for StarKist, even though
Charlie himself no doubt could have sung some killer a cappella.

No *Yum, yum, Bumblebee! Bumblebee Tuna!* No *Ask any mermaid you happen to see, 'What's the best tuna?' 'Chicken of the Sea.'* Bumblebees, fish-women, chicken-tuna hybrids—if that's what I had to work with, maybe I'd try a little buoyant music too.

Instead of music to his ears, Charlie heard the same voice over and over in his more than eighty TV commercial appearances: *StarKist doesn't want tunas with good taste. StarKist wants tunas that taste good.* So Charlie's one of two things: resilient or dyslexic.

## iv.

That's more than eighty schemes a single tuna fish dreamed up to demonstrate the good taste he kept thinking StarKist wanted: classy musician, veteran world traveler, slingshot Abstract painter, interior decorator, breeder of thoroughbred sea horses. One time his annoying little sidekick fish found Charlie poring over one impossibly enormous book, and of course he had to ask, as if he really cared, *What's it about?* And Charlie didn't miss a beat: *It's not about nothin'. It's poetry.*

## v.

Charlie—the Outsider who desperately, most definitely wanted In.

## vi.

No one was immune to the rampant 1960s national paranoia: Vietnam, JFK, LBJ, MLK, RFK, Richard Milhous Nixon, and Vietnam again. Charlie's more personally disheartening variation: some preposterous inverted paranoia, worse with every passing day, that StarKist wasn't out to get him.

### vii.

The unseen StarKist trawler that kept Charlie hopping and hoping
was as powerfully unsatisfying as playwright Beckett's Godot—
Charlie will be in the same non-boat tomorrow, and when
that's exactly what happens, how much will he remember of today?
His dream is all but dead in the water, even if he doesn't see it
that way. The one thing he knows for certain is
he's still very much alive, and he's not sure what to do about that.

### viii.

I'm guessing that most of us, given the luxury of choosing, would
want what Charlie wanted. We'd rather be told *you have good taste*
than *you taste good*—although if we ever hear the other, let it come
from the lips of a lover we've had the good taste to take on.

### ix.

As for its own sense of taste, trading on Charlie's good name,
StarKist offered Charlie-the-Tuna merchandise galore:
alarm clocks and watches and bicycle radios;
pendants and cufflinks and earrings and cameras;
bathroom scales, telephones, coin banks, and lamps;
neckties and T-shirts and ball caps and beach towels
and best of all, Charlie-the-Tuna hi-ball glasses
and Charlie-the-Tuna lo-ball glasses, so that we might
better make ready to face another day's unfailing ups and downs.

### x.

His *Sorry, Charlie* rejection note was sent down every time
on a gigantic fish hook. Quickly it became one of the most
popular American catch-phrases of its day, embraced
by schoolkids, mobsters, and editors alike—a thanks-but-no-thanks
blow-off, or a watery apology at best.

After ad-man Rogers, 87,
drowned in his backyard swimming pool, everyone at his funeral
was thinking the same thing as the casket was lowered,
and one completely unself-conscious little girl with moxie
had the good sense to yell it out loud for all of them: *Sorry, Tommy!*

## xi.

The girl I was sweet on in second grade was traumatized
by my Disney comic book, wherein Donald Duck and his nephews
sit down to a supper of duck lovingly proffered by Donald's own
sweet Daisy. I tried explaining that what lay there on the platter was
a different order of duck entirely—the edible, non-wisecracking kind.
This was a dinner party, after all, and not the Donner Party.
Still, Charlie wouldn't be caught dead eating a tuna-salad sandwich.

## xii.

Advertising has always had its share of animals too gladly
serving up some version of themselves, no matter how obliquely:
hundreds of pigs on Southern highway billboards
shilling for barbeque joints. Chickens wholly unruffled, shamelessly
hawking their own less fortunate—drawn and quartered, battered
beyond barnyard recognition, then deep-sixed in the fryer.
Charlie never called such unwanted attention to others of his kind.
He tried to do whatever he could for his own greater glory. He was
that he was. Take him or leave him. All Charlie or nothing at all.

## xiii.

In his mind he'd been born to play the part—Charlie
the Tuna, the Chosen One, sort of an undersea Dalai Lama, but
minus the requisite humility and one more stubborn fact:
he was never chosen. After his forced retirement
StarKist slapped his likeness on their label—to keep him alive,

in a manner of corporate speaking. They'd always done
that much for him, although he'd never asked them to.
But by this time hardly anyone remembered who he was,
the household name he'd been, his steadfast animated dedication
to good taste. I'm sorry that it had to come to that, sorry
his inspired, misguided efforts now are all but lost. And even
in a lifetime full of more substantially regrettable occasions,
more than ever, I am unapologetically so very sorry, Charlie.

## Cryptozoology 101: The Academics Have a Point, and Yet Once Again They Miss a Much Larger One

If there are really creatures out there in the woods
that have largely succeeded in ducking us for thousands of years,
we'd be better off bumping into any of them
one at a time. That way, we might know what
to call it: *I saw, you saw, we saw Bigfoot.*
Two or more, and it's anybody's guess: *Bigfoot, Bigfoots,*
*Bigfeet were watching*—a nomenclature nightmare,
and the tabloids as usual are no help at all:
*I WAS RAISED BY A TRIBE OF BIGFEET!!*

*BIGFOOTS PLANNING WORLD DOMINATION!!*

*BIGFOOT CLAIM THEY'VE BEEN MISUNDERSTOOD!!*

*I HAD, YOU HAD, WE HAD A LONELY BIGFOOT'S LOVE-CHILD!!*

## Greetings from Roswell, New Mexico: Home of the Historic 1947 Flying Saucer Crash

**i.**

In this down-on-its-luck-after-World-War-II town, finally
they came to know a good thing when they saw it: the allure
of tourism, extraterrestrial-style. Roswell's back
in business on the national map—rezoned, a sudden metropolis
of possibilities. *Roswell*—now a recognized pop-culture mantra,
a word intoned to stand in for Whatever Happened There.
T-shirts, coffee mugs, and bumper stickers. Two museums
scant blocks apart, devoted completely to the crash
and all the ensuing UFO hubba-hubba. Limited-edition
commemorative tins of actual crash-site soil. Two local ranchers
each claiming to own the one-and-only stretch of land
where the saucer came down, exploding into mythic smithereens:
WHOLE-DAY ADMISSION: $10 or WILL YOU FIND A PIECE
THE GOVERNMENT CLEAN-UP MISSED? Either way,
this whole thing is certainly a stretch.

                    On anniversary weekends
there's a parade down Main Street. Folks dress up as friendly
almond-eyed aliens, or come tricked out as military brass—
or else it really *is* the military, there to crash the party
in their inimitable way. The high school band plays spirited,
corny arrangements of a few appropriate tunes: *Great Balls
of Fire*. Sheb Wooley's highflying *Purple People Eater*.
Their signature finale, *Wipe Out*. Rollicking right behind them

is the prize-winning Crashed Saucer float, composed this time
of chicken wire, aluminum foil, and Christmas lights in July.
And that's Miss Roswell, waving in the midst of the debris.

At this rate there's not a lot of room
for skeptics in the street: one kid in serious glasses
at the tail-end of the spectacle, buzzing away
on Buddy Holly's *That'll Be the Day*. But even at that,
it's a flying saucer kazoo. He's too young to believe
that no one's listening, that he might as well save his breath.

## ii.

In the name of research you might even get in the car
and drive yourself to Roswell, to Corona, to the desolate Plains
of San Agustin: a completely different planet.
You might truly think—despite the years that have flown by,
the multitude of people who have covered this same ground—
you've made it this far for a reason, an explanation if only
you could find that one piece everybody else left behind.
If you presumed anything less, you wouldn't be out there,
wouldn't be human, looking up against the incredible odds
for something falling from the sky one more time: some crazy
resilient answer you've been waiting for amid the detritus
of a lifetime, the psychic wreckage of those days
you felt yourself all at once going irretrievably to pieces.

You still have no Earthly idea what went down in 1947,
but you can feel it in the air. Something's always going down
where you can't see it. It's impossible to suppose
otherwise. Surely there's a chance you'll turn up eventually
at some new collusion's Ground Zero, amazingly In The Know
from the very start. On the other side of the questions for once
where now the only thing left for you to do is live long enough

to get it right, your rendition of exactly what happened.

And when they come with their attachés and their badges
to take that away from you, maybe you'll know better
how to do what you absolutely have to do again,
how to pick up even the least substantial pieces remaining
on the trail of the same old story: making it alive
through one more version of a day you can't begin
to answer for, if only you can find it in yourself. Or wherever
in the world, out of whatever blue it came from last time,
so unmistakably promising, to you.

# Because It Was the Year the Mayan Calendar Ran Out, Some People Feared the Worst in 2012

## i. How Far into the New Year Can We Still Say *Happy New Year*?

It truly comes as no surprise: the back-booth-at-White-Castle regulars
invoke the Mayan calendar over coffee, insisting also that aliens
will figure in this year's end of the world. It seems they've established
secret bases on the dark side of the Moon.

                                              In the next booth over
I'm thinking maybe that's why NASA's lately left the Moon alone.
The regulars would pity me for thinking we ever were actually there.

I really hope these guys are mistaken about the Mayan doom-and-gloom.
Clearly they could use a calendar with cheery outdoor scenes
or national monuments or any kind of women at all.

                                                 I need them inexplicably
still here a year from now: their own secret base on the bright side,
for once, in this life that hasn't gone completely wrong.

## ii. It's Surely Just a Little Ancient-Mayan Misunderstanding, but Still I Can't Help Feeling Slightly Anxious Today

*December 20, 2012—End-of-the-World Eve*

When the guy shooting hoops by himself on the playground
sees me watching him, he stops just long enough to holler
as if by way of introduction: *C'mon over, man—I'm a Walk
in the Park.* He says it again, and now it sounds a lot more like
*I'm a Walkin' Apocalypse.* If he's either one of those
he can't also be the other—not at the same time.
Speaking for myself, I'd much rather make that leisurely stroll
than take some horrible version of that final four-horse ride.

When he spins and shoots, it's nothing but net again.
Maybe he's only talking some sandlot trash. Maybe
I should tell him my name is Mr. You-Want-a-Piece-of-Me,
but I'd just as likely answer to Mr. I'm-a-Piece-of-Cake. I am
one sweet accident waiting to happen, either way.

And while the two of us are standing around and waiting for
who knows what, exactly, a car runs a red light down the street,
hurtling through the intersection. And now the obligatory horn,
some screeching brakes, but thankfully this time no deadening
*thunk* of metal on metal—merely one more close call of so many
in the daily ragtag parade of hit-and-miss where it's a matter
of luck having its way with all of us, for better or for worse.

As long as we're both still remarkably here in the day's last light—
which might at the same time just this once turn out to be
the last day's light as well—I suggest a quick game of Around
the World. I can tell by the look on his face that he'd rather go
one-on-one, but there's no way I'm about to let that happen.

Lofting another offhand wonder of a shot, he says *Okay, but*
*care to make it interesting?* and I say *Sure, why not?* although
I'm thinking today there's already plenty that's interesting,
given all the nutty Mayan hoopla in the air. There are really people
hunkered down in their homemade bunkers right now, and others
up on mountaintops where alien saucers can find them with ease
if need be, take them off the planetary grid in an instant.
But my accommodating basketball friend doesn't seem too worried.

So let's hope there's time enough yet for a little easier going.
Even a small piece of cake or a short walk in the park
would be so much better than nothing. Yeah, I'll probably lose big
and wind up ten bucks lighter, but I swear: before it's over, whenever
it's over, I will go down smiling if it's the last thing I do.

# The JFK Assassination Deluxe Diorama Kits Are Here!

*Did our 35th president fall victim to a disgruntled lone nut,
or to a national, or even international, cabal made up
of two or more of the following elements: Texas oilmen, the CIA,
mobsters, Fidel Castro, Cuban exiles, Nikita Khrushchev, or even
his own vice president? After all this time, you're the one
who decides. Have it your way! Create your very own
lifelike death-at-high-noon assassination scenarios!*

❂ ❂ ❂ ❂ ❂ ❂ ❂ ❂

Thank you for choosing the *Lee Harvey Oswald Special Edition.*
Please consider owning our other fine kits as well—while supplies last:

*The Parkland Hospital Scenario Kit*, with the famously well-traveled
pristine Magic Bullet, the stretcher where it was unbelievably discovered,
and the Secret Service agents who shot down the Dallas autopsy;

*The* Air Force One *LBJ-Swearing-In Scenario Kit*, with
Let's-Get-This-Show-on-the-Road LBJ, the widow Jackie, Ladybird,
Judge Sarah Hughes, and JFK tucked safely away in his temporary casket;

*The Bethesda Naval Hospital Official Autopsy Scenario Kit*,
with reversible exit-wound/entrance-wound decals and transfers,
as well as a portfolio of doctored drawings, photos, and reports.

❂ ❂ ❂ ❂ ❂ ❂ ❂ ❂

Your *Lee Harvey Oswald Special Edition Kit* includes
built-to-scale models of these historic Dealey Plaza landmarks:

the Texas School Book Depository, Dal-Tex Building,
Triple-Overpass, and Grassy Knoll with Stockade Fence.
(Presidential limousine with detachable bubble-top,
Secret Service agents, Dallas motorcycle policemen, Abraham
"The Movie Man" Zapruder, flag-waving onlookers, and
possible French contract assassins each sold separately.)

But the focus here, unquestionably, is on Lee Harvey Oswald.
Historically, he's always had so many places to go and
people to see and, too often, so little time. Just look
at the different Oswalds he's been! Chances are he's not merely
an innocent bystander right now either, for the first time in his life.
With the two-dozen die-cast little Oswalds in this kit,
you can re-create all the actual Oswalds you can handle
from before, during, or immediately after his Dealey Plaza doings.
Go ahead! Put each one of them in motion at once!
Under your watchful eye, it's every Oswald for himself:

New-York-City-teenage-truant-at-the-Bronx-Zoo Oswald,
fan-of-Cold-War-TV's-*I-Led-3-Lives*-but-who's-counting Oswald,
*Semper-Fi*-at-17-who's-memorized-both-the-*Marine-Corps-Manual*-
and-*Das-Kapital*-entirely Oswald, more-capable-Marxist-than-
marksman Oswald, Atsugi-Japan-Air-Base-U2-spy-plane-radar-man-
and-CIA-MK-ULTRA'd-psychotropic Oswald,
nearly-two-years-of-living-well-in-not-so-well-off-Russia Oswald,
in-some-kind-of-love-with-Russian-bride-Marina Oswald, renouncing-
U.S.-citizenship-and-then-renouncing-the-renunciation Oswald,
New-Orleans-*Fair-Play-for-Cuba*-leafleteering-pro-Castro Oswald,
schmoozing-in-the-Cuban-exiles'-living-room-anti-Castro Oswald,
snacks-at-the-Cuban-and-Russian-embassies-in-Mexico-City Oswald,
landing-a-job-in-less-than-a-day-at-the-Book-Depository Oswald—

*remember: no one's saying he's not involved at all.*
*His whole life he's been nothing if not involved—*

ramshackle-Ruth-Paine-rooming-house Oswald,
backyard-revolutionary-pasted-photo Oswald,
fifteen-dollar-mail-order-rifle Oswald, curtain-rods Oswald,
second-floor-breakroom-calmly-drinking-soda Oswald,
walking-home Oswald, bus-transfer Oswald, taxi-cab Oswald,
what's-Officer-J.D.-Tippit-stopping-him-for Oswald,
Texas-Theater-arrested-during-*War-Is-Hell* Oswald,
police-station Oswald, guessing-he's-been-set-up-as-the-patsy Oswald,
after-hours-of-interrogation-where-are-the-notes Oswald,
handcuffed-to-a-nervous-Detective-Leavelle Oswald, going-down-
in-the-elevator-going-down Oswald, point-blank Oswald,
shot-in-the-gut-by-Jack-Ruby Oswald,
and being-rushed-too-late-to-Parkland-just-like-JFK Oswald—

*remember: no one's saying he didn't have this coming.*
*No one's saying he didn't see this coming.*

o o o o o o o o o

Oswald's been hurrying all over the place, and in a single hour
the city of Dallas will be all over Oswald. Two more days and,
no matter what else happens, it will be all over finally for Oswald.
No one's saying there's no way he knew a thing about this.
No one's saying he would have been acquitted by a jury, but
if you don't put him in the sixth-floor window, then that's that:
he isn't in the window. No one could put him there for certain
on the day in question either. There's no doubt he's seen
a world of hurt and oddball wonder in his twenty-four young years,
but if he hasn't watched a motorcade from six floors up,
then it's possible he hasn't seen anything yet. And if
he's really sniper's-nested in the window, does he have a rifle?
Does he fire it? That's up to you. No one's quite saying he didn't.
If he hears another gun reporting, is he panicked, or relieved?

**38**

And when does it finally occur to him that *now* he knows
what's going down—or knows at least enough to be dangerous
at last, still alive and on the loose in the Dallas streets?

It's your decision! You're the one who's bought and paid for him
this time. He'll show up where you ask him to. He'll be
the Oswald you want him to be. In fact he'd consider it
some small kind of cockeyed honor, and for the life of him
at this late date, he wouldn't have it any other way.

◦ ◦ ◦ ◦ ◦ ◦ ◦ ◦ ◦

*Final Caution:*

*Some assembly required—okay, some* considerable *assembly.*
*Do not force pieces together. Do not force pieces into place.*
*Some parts are incredibly small and by all means*
*should be kept out of the reach of children—as should*
*the official conclusions of the* Warren Commission Report
*which, if swallowed, constitute an even greater choking hazard.*

## What If All Along We've Been Wrong About Tinfoil Hats

**i.**

and they're not quite everything they've been cracked up to be,
so instead of rendering the wearer impervious
to government-sanctioned mind manipulation or any other
mental interference whatsoever—thereby allowing us to keep
our thoughts and only our thoughts to ourselves, under
our control alone, inviolable and whole—these hats in fact
are amplifying certain signals from the outside, making tinfoil more
or less the unofficial headwear of state-supported confusion,
and we who have been so conscientious, so downright vigilant,
wake up one day to discover our station as hapless government dupes
or worse, the unwitting pawns of our alien overlords on Earth
paving the way for an invasion guaranteed to meet with absolutely
no resistance, thanks to these hats that enhance the power
of whoever wants inside our heads to get there without fail,

these hats that were supposed to protect us by repelling all manner
of radio frequencies, microwaves, electrical impulses that might otherwise
alter chemicals in the brain, reconfigure the hard-wiring already
jerrybuilt at best—these hats can't even fend off late-night-radio talk shows,
TV evangelists, ABBA songs, those pitches from personal-injury lawyers,
or the ceaseless chatter of once-distant relatives suddenly in our living rooms,
so what chance did we have against professional electromagnetic distortion
or hypno-assassination programming, Manchurian-Candidate-style,
or someone imprinting the latest revision of the New World Order agenda,
let alone the incessant national elevator music piped in to insure
a softened-up population, grown somehow more docile than ever?

## ii.

At the height of the Cold War, government spooks were all over
this idea of *Electromagnetic Hearing*—headgear that would *facilitate
covert message reception* for people they knew to be on our side
but also might *function as a nonlethal weapon of disruption
by inducing voices in the enemy's head*, as if said enemy really could
be talked into wearing so ridiculous a thing in the first place.
In those exhilarating years of nearly giddy R&D,
it was never about keeping any voices out. They were looking for surefire
ways to sneak the voices farther *in*. And so they spread the disinformative
opposite word entirely—*a reliable defensive posture*—then sat back
and waited for the tinfoil hats to start showing up in the streets: tinfoil
beanies, tinfoil fedoras, tinfoil hunting caps with tinfoil earflaps—genuine
American ingenuity at work, no matter how profoundly misguided.

But my Uncle Bud, whose middle name was usually Misguided Ingenuity,
wasn't falling for the hats. This was a man forever extending
the reach of his ancient TV's wobbling rabbit-ears with tinfoil—
his very own precarious Super-Antenna. His one and only Herculean labor.
He suspected such hats would make matters much worse—they were nothing
but indiscriminate receivers wide open to a world full of trouble—
and Bud was a man who surely knew his way around a roll of foil.
He insisted we'd be better off just putting our fingers in our ears,
closing our eyes, and singing at the top of our lungs in the dark again,
drowning out voices we'd rather not hear with a favorite TV-show theme song
over and over. He was partial to *The Flintstones* because it seemed to promise
that if we choose more carefully the company we keep, there might be
brighter days ahead: *a yabba-dabba-doo time* could yet possibly be had,
but *a dabba-doo time* at the very least.

## iii.

If you're still attached to the idea of a hat, consider a material
more innocuous than tinfoil. Maybe you could fold yourself an old-fashioned
newspaper hat—something you never before saw the point of, really, even
in kindergarten. No tough guy, no hero, no self-respecting neighborhood kid
could afford to be caught dead in such a flimsy get-up, but then again,
you always knew what you were getting into. When you put on a hat
like that, there weren't any crazy expectations. So why not go ahead
and fashion a cardboard sword while you're at it? There could be
someone who will actually assume that you're not afraid to use it, either.

And if it should rain, yes, you'll be waterlogged, completely soaked
to the skin, but where's the serious harm in that? Chances are you'll live
to fight another day. A tinfoil hat's a different story altogether, the last thing
you need in rough weather. It tends to call the lightning down. Better to be
a make-believe sailor or pirate who's managed to ride out one more storm—
good news anyone can see for themselves in the ink running down your face.
And no one's about to tell you anything you haven't already thought of
on your own—even if you can't always seem to remember for certain
what gave you that idea to begin with.

# II.

# Civility Was All the Rage

° ° ° ° ° ° ° ° °

*henceforth call me Snarl*
*I belong to my teeth*
*I live where I sit*

*you will set me a place at your table*
*cut me a key of my own*
*henceforth I will go when I please*
*in or out*

—Donald Finkel, "For Every Dog"

## Do Not Overinflate

Until the first time I came across those actual words,
it's nothing I ever would have thought of doing, not once—
and, frankly, never would have known was even possible.
But the pointed nature of the warning made me suddenly
self-conscious, turned me from then on into a living,
breathing wreck: what if my next breath or pumpful of air
were the one to cause whatever I was huffing and puffing
to burst, to fly apart at the seams, to be blown out of
all shapely proportion? This printed insistence was a bad idea
that really should have gone forever without saying:

on the ridiculously shallow backyard kiddie pool
with its six inches of water getting warmer by the minute
until it's nearly simmering under the summer afternoon sun;

on the ubiquitous hard-red-rubber kickball, that harsh *boing*
echoing when it smacked inevitably into someone's unsuspecting face
on the red-dirt grade-school playground of small indignities;

on the tires of that classic '59 Schwinn, aqua with gold trim,
fenders like Cadillac fins, the coolest ride by far
my clunky self would ever almost manage to pull off;

on the mail-order Female Companion—more scary than even
remotely sexy—that I filled with helium to see how far she'd go
into the Newark sky, and in the next day's *Star-Ledger* she's a UFO story;

on each of the worn-down radials holding up the ancient Ford Escort
that to this day, and against all reasonable automotive odds,
somehow gets me unfailingly where I still need to go;

on the life rafts that even right now are being lowered all over,
and quickly, into one more day's choppy waters,
where so far any blood's just metaphorical, and so too, for now, the sharks.

With whatever we've tried breathing some honest portion of ourselves into—
jobs, friendships, marriages, recovery programs—
it's as if, had we not been repeatedly warned, we never would have known
when to stop: *Do not overinflate.* At a certain point,
like the CPR that turns out so often to be not nearly enough to rescue anyone,
we might as well have saved our breath for the next time
we were sure to need it again, might as well have kept on going,
walking away still under anything that's left of our own power.

# In 1963 I Had to Write a Thousand Words

and not just any thousand words, but what Miss Higgins called
an *essay*—the first time in my grade-school life I'd heard
that dreaded word—explaining how at last I'd learned
my lesson: no more disruptions in her classroom, no more
*talking out of turn*, as if whatever I had to say was by far
more important than what any other kid was coming up with.

And I remember thinking at the time how a thousand
of anything had to be a lot: a thousand miles, a thousand years,
a thousand pieces of Bazooka. So, really—a thousand words
in a row? After school Miss Higgins said that if I chose
to write a poem instead, well maybe then she wouldn't bother
counting up the words. She figured that my trying any poem,
no matter how long it was or wasn't, would prove undoubtedly
to be punishment enough. Yes, I was young but wasn't stupid—
I took the poem. And no, it wasn't very good, but at least
Debbie Fuller was in it, and I have to say I liked that part.

Fifty years later I still haven't learned. I'm still talking
out of turn and insisting on poems—every one of them asking,
in so many words: punishment for *whom*? Miss Higgins
of the Thousand Words, Miss Higgins of the Fiendish Plan B,
are you there? I've even written poems a thousand words long
and longer, but not this one—you and I had a deal.
My uncompromising reader, reader there at the beginning,
never less than tough on me—what I really want to know is
have you had enough yet?

# In 1966 Debbie Fuller Was Sweet on Pluto

*To be classified as a planet, a celestial object must meet three requirements: it orbits the Sun; it has gravity enough to have formed and maintained a spherical shape; and it must have cleared other bodies out of the way in its orbital neighborhood.*

—new criteria for planets, as decided by the International
Astronomical Union (2006)

At Hamilton Elementary, forty years before Pluto lost its planetary status,
there was just one small mistake in Debbie Fuller's solar system.
Typically a ten-year-old stickler for the scientific method, this time
she couldn't help herself: she gave her favorite planet floppy ears,
assuming like so many that it had been named in 1930
for Mickey Mouse's dog, and not for the Roman god of the dead.
Otherwise, hers was a fragile, Styrofoam thing of exacting beauty.

Her planets were proportionately sized, and 33 moons
were in all the right places. The Sun at the center held everything together
with nine thin rods jutting out at different lengths. Each moon
had a wire of its own standing in for home-planet gravity. And somehow
her mother hauled it in the back of her station wagon to school,
where 43 spray-painted polystyrene orbs arrayed with such precision
took up a version of real space in that classroom already brimming
with our more ho-hum poster-board depictions. Debbie Fuller had gone 3-D
in a big way, had gone to her own great lengths. And all I could manage
was my usual shy grin—more pronounced whenever I found myself
in her gravitational pull—and something about my liking Pluto too,
despite that unfortunate Disney dog/ruler-of-the-underworld confusion.

Fueled by a couple of Lucky Strikes, janitor Geiss ascended his ladder
and hung the whole sprawling shebang from the ceiling
where it stayed for most of the school year, until that fateful day
in the middle of Blob Rosenberg's impassioned oral report—JFK's assassination,
flying saucers, or some other nuttiness he'd lately been enthralled by—
when the solar system came undone. Our fifth-grade sky was falling,
wafting and clattering down at once in a commotion of Styrofoam.
Celestial bodies disengaged from the Sun, rolling haphazardly
out of their orbits. The gravity of what had just happened
brought us to our knees, where maybe we could better see
what we were looking for.

          Soon each planet and moon was rediscovered,
except for Pluto, which anyway had always been marginal at best.
We did what we could by way of rod-and-wire reconstruction,
but when Geiss eventually put it back up in its makeshift firmament,
it all seemed more lopsided, more wobbly than before. And now
there were only eight planets—an accidental reassessment
far ahead of its time. Debbie Fuller would have been distraught,
but she'd moved away a few months earlier, leaving the solar system
entirely behind. So we left it there too, hanging over our weary heads
in her honor, even beyond the last day of school.

She couldn't have known how much we thought about it, how much
some of us clearly thought of her. It's hard saying anything like that
out loud when you're ten, when you barely realize who you are.
I hope she knows how lucky she was to be in fifth grade
so long before the current lunar count: a staggering 166 moons.
She'd be lugging her creation to school on a flatbed trailer.
And wherever she is out there today, she surely has to know
that her beloved Pluto didn't go down in real life
without an astronomical fight: *My Very Energetic Mother
Just Served Us Nine . . . what?!* But I hope she never heard it

dismissed in the end as a ball of rock and ice no bigger than Texas,
just another pale face in the crowded Kuiper Belt—a zone
of frozen debris beyond Neptune.

        Pluto's downfall turned out to be
the last of the Astronomical Union's conditions: that a planet must
be able to clear out its orbital neighborhood—although
on a Friday in April of 1966, when it seemed as if nothing could
deliver us from the Blob's inscrutable theories, it happened:
for at least a few minutes, Pluto was as good as its planetary word.

Exactly how that dog-eared planet wound up in my pocket
is not a mystery. I looked down after lunch, and there
it was. And I would take care of Pluto for her, forever—
that kind of swearing's not unseemly when you're ten.
Now, more than forty years later, after losing track of so much
time, so many moons and planets, and even whatever it was
about Debbie Fuller, I'd like to think that maybe somewhere
in the neighborhood of this woefully unscientific poem,
I'm still doing anything I can to keep that promise.

# In the Extreme

I was young when I first experienced the danger of extremes—
what later on I'd come to know by their familiar names: feast
or famine, hell or high water, all or nothing's wide variety
of guises and occasions. I learned that lesson over and over
at my family's bathroom sink, so unlike any other sink
I'd ever stood before—hot-water faucet on the left,
cold-water faucet on the right. I found out early on
that neither one of those alone was going to suffice, so I tried
flitting my hands back and forth, pausing in the middle,
hoping for anything easier to weather—not-so-tropical heat,
not-so-icy Arctic Circle—but no compromise seemed possible.
I could stare into the mirror, stalling for time, but again
and again I had to choose between *Hot* on the one hand
and *Cold* on the other.
                        Even Hamlet's self-absorbed dilemma
was a cinch, compared to mine. Yes, *not to be* was surely
an extreme, but maybe just a bit dramatic too, considering
his princely circumstances. All he really had to do was be.
And as for *the thousand natural shocks that flesh is heir to*?
I bet he never had to reckon with the same two every morning
of his life before breakfast. To be scalded or not scalded—that
was always the more immediately worrisome question.

And when my parents finally updated, in that one small way
at least, I oddly came to miss the regular hand-wringing over
how best to carry out my daily perilous ablutions.

My father's luck with home repairs ran hot and cold, but
one morning he led me to the sink, where the water was running
from a single, shining faucet. It had taken him all night,
but he'd banged and hacked and wrenched us that much further
into the twentieth century: *You don't need to use
a stopper anymore!* A stopper? A stopper—and I was suddenly
mortified in the extreme. I watched what I'd taken for so long
as my own tepid sense of accomplishment circling the drain,
gurgling on its way down out of sight.

# My Father's Wholehearted Mixed Message

*You can have too much of a good thing, you know,*
my father was fond of declaring—as if he knew, as if
something like that had happened to him even once.
From where I stood at age ten, he never seemed to have
enough—free time, easy money, some kind of credit
where credit was due. Too much trouble was another thing
completely. He could have been all over that, the way it was
all over him—tedious job, unreliable car, mortgage on his back
the size of the sleek Buick he never would be able to afford.
But he didn't want to let any of that be a lesson to me.

He had the good love of my mother, though—and luckily
he knew there was no such thing, ever, as too much of that.
And when it came to her, which he made sure it did
every day of their lives, he absolutely gave as good as he got.
Still, when he felt obliged to impart a share of fatherly wisdom,
his caution against all manner of excess—chili-cheese-dogs,
consecutive snow days, or kissing Debbie Fuller on her
preternaturally full-fledged grade-school lips—he thought
it was always such a good thing to say that he couldn't possibly
stop himself from saying it way too much.

He'd never heard of Shakespeare's bawdy good-thing pun
in Act 4, scene 1 of *As You Like It*. And neither had my mother,
although she took to quoting Mae West's salacious version
and let my father have it more than once: *Too much of a good thing
can be wonderful.* She was trying hard to set the good-thing record

straight for both of them, and while my father undoubtedly
appreciated that, he wasn't about to put it quite that way to me.

I was young and so wide open then. Those were the days
I took everything too much to heart. He tried his best to teach me
when to say enough's enough—a sense of moderation that came
much too easily to him because what other choice did he have.
But the only thing I learned instead was the unswerving
saving grace of love, whether I was ready for it, finally, or not.

# I'm Sorry There Are No More *Flying Saucers*

These days everything is a *UFO* instead:
military stealth planes and flying triangles, satellites
and meteorites, suborbital space debris, the planet Venus
and Chinese lanterns attached to a horde of helium balloons—
hell, sometimes even my unlikely Uncle Bud,
lit up and soaring after a few too many again, until finally
he's recognized by someone who will see him the long way home.
It used to be when you said *flying saucer*,

you meant a nuts-and-bolts machine that had come to Earth
from somewhere else, and Bud never would have been confused
for anything like that—he'd been down-to-Earth forever,
as homegrown as they come. And there's no way he'd ever be
onboard for even a minute with beings whose brightest idea
was invariably some version of *Take me to your leader*, which
always led to Bud shaking his head. He knew a bad idea
when he heard it, and he wasn't about to believe
this flying saucer business had anything to do with
the likelihood of intelligent life anywhere else in the universe.

# Even After All This Time, I'd Like to Have a Word with You

*for who else but Patricia*

## i.

It would be our very own word again, a word
no one else can use. It could be
a fancy word, a naughty word,
a magic word, or maybe a proverbial word
to the wise, if only we knew what that meant.
It wouldn't have to be an elegant word,
set forever in polished stone. It might be
a fixer-upper word, some on-the-spur-of-
the-moment word, or a word with crazy flyaway hair.

And it's likely any *this* would lead to a definite
*that*, until we're somewhere almost beyond words—
as if that could really happen. Not with both of us
so wedded to our stubborn ways with them.
We'd want still another word, and then another
until it's one more complicated story we can't help
making up, word by word, as we go along.
It's not as much about what happens next
as what, exactly, is happening right now—
the kind of story that's totally lost on children.
This is a story for adults, but it might
not be quite what you're thinking. Say instead it flirts
with jealousy, greed, even unintentional cruelty, and
none of these are words I ever want to have with you.

I want something tender to sink my teeth into.
I want something sweet on the tongue.
I'll try to refrain from putting words in your mouth,
but do you know any words like these,
and will you please have one of them with me?

## ii.

We always mean to be as good as our word,
but sometimes that's just asking for it, I'm afraid.
If you give me yours, I'll give you mine—
a grown-up version of that unnerving grade-school offer,
half dare and half promise. Those were the days
when words themselves were constantly a problem:

*A train leaves from the station at Point A,*
*traveling 70 mph for the first half of the trip*
*to the station at Point B, then 60 mph for an hour*
*and a half, then 50 mph the rest of the way.*
*And don't ask why the train keeps slowing down.*
*If the distance between stations is a thousand miles,*
*how long does it take to get to the Point-B station?*

The real problem all along, of course, easier
to see now from this distance: who cares, without you
anywhere on board? You were so far in the future
that I never saw you coming
or I would have done everything in my small power
to meet you at whatever station, no matter how many
miles, how many years later. I would have waited
for you to tell me in your own words why
it took you so long finally to arrive.

## My Teenage Son Is Lately Preoccupied with Textiles

*for Ben, who might as well have written this*

On his way out the door, not quite running
late for his first date with the girl from English class
after weeks of working up the nerve just to ask her,
he tugged at the collar of his brand-new shirt and said he bet
I didn't know what kind of fabric it was. I'm not much of a
discerning-fabric-kind-of-guy, and surely he'd have to forgive
my scattershot guesses: *Cotton? Silk? Flannel? Gabardine?*

Combing his hair in the rearview mirror, he hollered at me
through his rolled-down window: *Gabber-what? That last one
sounded really cool, but I was going for* boyfriend material.

# The Bartender Doesn't Ask Much

*Don't talk religion or politics with the bartender. If you must talk to the bartender,*
*make it baseball.*

      —homemade sign taped to the back-bar mirror

## i.

That's why, in such a volatile era, it's absolutely refreshing to hear
this nutty guy pushing his luck with the bartender—in the same breath,
defying both of those posted prohibitions each time he loudly falls back on
his nearly unwavering credo: *Believe what you will, but I believe*
*I'll have another drink if you please, O Most Respected Publican*—the same routine over
and over, if not for his closing, which dubs the bartender *Good Sheriff,* then
*Your Majesty,* then *My Fearless Leader.* I never see him with anything less
than the strength of his liquid conviction, faith so palpable there's no doubt
he'll be up all night trying to relieve himself of its wondrous burden.

Everyone in the place immediately wants a piece of this guy's brazen action.
They've become effusive, taboo-braving devotees, as in *What's*
*with the Pope's hat* and *I can't go to Hell if it's merely a state of mind* and
*Why do we need a state poet laureate when real jobs are disappearing?*
Well, *if the governor can't balance the budget, at least he's got someone who*
*can make it rhyme.* Now the whole room's laughing except the bartender, naturally,
who can't help thinking, seriously, that the guy who started this brouhaha
was flouting House Rules—his handwritten, taped-up sense of decorum—not to mention
conventional taproom wisdom everywhere.

                         And just when he's guessing
he should probably ask this guy to leave, Mister True Believer throws down
more cash on the bar. Tonight he's taking care of everyone's beliefs,
proclaiming that Jesus was assuredly right about the money-changers, and

Shakespeare too, when he made his farsighted, let's-kill-all-the-lawyers suggestion, *but hey, what's not to like about the Cardinals this year?* And finally the bartender has to admit there's no disagreeing with any of that.

## ii.

But he didn't want to hear about the goddamn New York Mets:
*I could care less—I really could.* What he meant, of course,
was that he *couldn't—really couldn't.* Care less,
I mean. Technically speaking, I suppose he could have cared less
when it came to his hometown St. Louis Cardinals,
whose hat was perched on top of his 350-easy pounds,
and about whom he cared perhaps a bit more than he should,
if his voice getting louder through his shortness of breath
was any indication.

           For a moment I thought I could tell him
precisely the error of two of his ways, at least. But my healthy concern
for his size and his general disposition suggested I probably
shouldn't. I mean, of course, that I *couldn't.* Tell him what he'd meant
to say, that is. Or I wouldn't, just then, if I were you
and you'd been there instead of me, that close to undoing Mr. 350-easy,
his face flushed as red as his beloved Cardinals. That close
to the baseball bat he kept behind the bar,
signed on the fattest part of the barrel by Stan the Man Musial himself.

# Buskers Forewarned

*We just want peace and tranquility in the right of way.*
—St. Louis Streets Department director, on holding auditions as
part of street performers' city-permit applications

*Instrumentalists:*
Something tuneful—no improvisations.
Real instruments only. No accordions.

*Singers:*
No TV-show theme songs or meaningless-dream songs,
and *The Wreck of the Edmund Fitzgerald*'s too long.

*Dancers:*
No Watusi. No Frug. No Locomotion.
No limbo stick lower than eighteen inches.

*Balloon-Twisters:*
No squeaking. No popping. None of the usual animals.
Try Bigfoot, Loch Ness Monster, Chupacabras, or Reptilians.

*Puppeteers:*
Nothing more risqué than where your two hands
are waiting to meet every puppet demand.

*Mimes:*
No. No
to infinity: no.

*Living Statues:*
No obvious twitching
or subtle foot-switching.

*Contortionists:*
Solo acts exclusively—no ensembles or duets,
no awkward or compromising positions in which to get.

*Jugglers:*
No chainsaws, fire, or knives.
No lovers and husbands or wives.

*Magicians:*
No pulling quarters from the ear of a single pedestrian.
No unsolicited shuffling. No gratuitous levitation.

*Fortunetellers:*
Tell folks at least a couple things they might not know already.
Go light on heartbreak, death, Republican presidents ahead.

*Caricaturists:*
It's not hard making people a bit bigger than they are.
What's hard is making people any better than they are.

*Poets:*
Collect no tips for verse. It's got to be free. And no haiku.
Heroic or not, no couplets—or else no busking for you.

# If We Were to Experience an Outbreak Like That One in Ancient Thrace

*(ca. 300 BCE)*

> *The good people of Abdera were seized with a violent fever for seven days,*
> *when some were relieved by a copious discharge of blood from the nostrils, and*
> *others by as plentiful a flow of sweat. Though the fever left them, some extraor-*
> *dinary and whimsical effects were produced. Their minds became so enchanted*
> *that they roared out iambics, and uttered all in recitative. Euripides was much*
> *intoned: "Love, cruel king of God and men" was one of the fine flourishes*
> *which these heroes sounded forth, without ceasing.*
>     —Lucian of Samosata

All at once those Thracians were afflicted with good taste,
the rich words of Euripides ringing out for days, and with no warning
everyone's a tragedian. But in our place and time,
when almost no one in the street knows any poetry—
although many would without a doubt admit to writing
poems of their own—I'm sorry to say there would be
no airborne Dickinson, no Whitman, no William Carlos Williams.
No Frost or Stevens, no Bishop or Ginsberg or Moore. Not even
the ghost of a nosebleed that might bring on T.S. Eliot.
Nothing outsized and necessarily tragic, in language melodic enough
for a chorus of sympathetic Greeks. That cruel king, love,
would be reduced to the harmlessly familiar—one more listless prince
with no designs on any throne. Flat lines of purported verse
would stack up in the deadening air, and breathing won't be easy:
*My Persian is an awfully pretty cat.*
*My father used to drink, and then he left.*
*I saw a washed-up starfish on the shore.*

Having endured the dullest of pains and common aches
for a week or for the better part of a lifetime,
our self-styled poets might believe some long, dry spell is broken.
And the only collective delusion left to suffer
will be little more than this: that they've actually lived
to tell about it. And since they have some kind of gift,
who are they to keep that to themselves, saying
and saying the same small thing in so many words again,
no sweat—another halfhearted squall of feeling
with no real blood or thunder in it.
                                        And who am I, exactly,
to claim I've courted a fever of any more epic proportion?
*I'm Nobody! Who are you?* and
*I too am not a bit tamed, I too am untranslatable* and
*This Is Just To Say*
that I'll be carrying on like this until finally I've got it:
a private audience with that unruly and powerful king
so exalted by deluded Thracians. Or else
please take any future significant bleeding on my part
as a sign of a loyal subject who's still trying.

# The Doctor's Wife

*9 Ridge Road*
*Rutherford, New Jersey*

## i. Her Plums Are Gone, and Flossie Williams Has Just This to Say

*How I wish that*
*my doctor*
*would be in*
*more often*

*instead*
*of improbably*
*starving*
*for art*

*Forget it—*
*who'll ever read his*
*excuse*
*for a poem?*

## ii. Okay—Flossie Williams Has Just One More Thing to Say to Her Husband: *I See That I Can't Depend*

*so much on you*
*to take*

*the red wheel*
*barrow*

*back to the shed*
*before*

*it rusts away*
*completely.*

# Too Far This Time

*Never trust a poet at the wheel.*
   —Martin Amis, *The Information*

*for Donald Finkel (1929–2008)*

You were at your very best on foot,
never missing a step as you kept walking, always
thinking on your feet, your hands completely free
to animate the words you coaxed out of one more day's thin air.
A born pedestrian on the move.
        If there was anywhere
we had to go that wasn't walking distance, I was the one
who said *I'll drive.* You'd be relieved again, a natural
riding shotgun. And so we made it every time:
to Santoro's or the races or hot jazz or Pizza-a-Go-Go,
to another far-flung poetry reading at Why-Do-They-Want-Us U.

But most of all, I see you walking through your life
to the north through the woods near Holy Smoke, Vermont.
To the south in the hills above San Miguel, and still farther south
in Antarctica, where you carried the geologists' ice-cold water
just for the chance to write postcards from the South Pole.
Even that far away from the rest of the world, you weren't
about to drive. You knew better back East, too—your phantom
Bronx, where you first learned what it meant to walk.

I'll see you forever walking in St. Louis, this town
that somehow passed for your idea of the Wild West:
the U. City Loop at high noon, gunsmoke along the River Despair,

and your last-stand routine: Lafayette Park, visiting Willie,
the swan that lived there for as long as he could—*strangely
gentle*, you said. *For a swan.* You couldn't believe
your luck: this unlikely friendship. But it was something
more than that, my odd-duck, rare-bird friend.

○ ○ ○ ○ ○ ○ ○ ○ ○

Finkel-at-the-Wheel-of-the-VW-Van was already
the stuff of local legend. Forgive me when I say I'm glad
that was a legend mostly before my own St. Louis time.
Thirty years ago, when you first walked into my apartment,
Woody Guthrie's *Car Song* was spinning out its final notes.
You stood there at attention, laughing: *Did I just hear
my national anthem?* You had to cue it up once more:
*Take me riding in the car, car. Take me riding
in the car, car.* You and me and Woody, raucous all together.
We talked into the dark, luxurious part of morning—then
one last chorus: *I'm a-gonna take you home again.
I'm a-gonna take you home again.* Riding in my car,

with the lone-but-gigantic exception of those 1,600 miles
to Mexico, summer 1995. You insisted on the driver's seat:
*I know exactly how to get there, man.* Connie—regardless
of your mode of locomotion, your unwavering compass, love
of your life—was stubbornly back-seat driving up front.
And in the true back seat, where I hadn't been much
since Jersey childhood, I hunkered down with Patricia,
the love of mine. Fearing for ours, although we couldn't say so.
Each night's hotel was a sanctuary with a bed
we never wanted to get out of the next morning. To be driven
stir-crazy again in Spanish: *Alto, Don, alto.* But once you got going,
it was always hard for you to stop.

○ ○ ○ ○ ○ ○ ○ ○ ○ ○

I wish I could have driven you to the Great Beyond
and back—especially back. It's always seemed to be a place
more out-of-the-way than it probably is. And I
wouldn't have known exactly how to get there.
I wish I could have heard you say *It wasn't really all
that great, man.*

                        You've gone too far this time, old friend.
Beyond where I can pick you up and steer you home
alive again. And here I am, driving myself a little nutty
thinking of you so irretrievably departed. I'm driving myself,
talking for us both. And it's just not the same.

# Here's to the Moon: Goodbye

## i. The Problem and the Promise

Great. Just great. As if there haven't been enough already:
another poem about the Moon—an idea whose time has surely come
and gone at least a thousand years ago. So why,
after centuries beneath the manhandled literary Moon,
do we still insist on gazing up in its direction, looking hard into
the lunar matter just once more? Why on Earth is anyone still
writing down the Moon, as if there might be some different light
that no one's thought to see it in before? Keats considered the Moon
a *maker of sweet poets*, but look around—there's no way he wasn't
out of his mind with the fever.

                               Maybe it's because we're made up
of so much salt water that leaks out gradually over a lifetime
of bleeding, sweating, coming, and crying, and we can't help
but acknowledge the pull of gravity having its stubborn way with us.
It's our humble tip-of-the-mortal-fedora, a gesture that survives
from a time when such civility was all the rage.
I've done my small part on so many occasions, and right about now
I'd love for this to be the last poem about the Moon—like it
or not. But if that's not to be, if ever I should weaken and find myself
inexplicably up to my neck again in some fat full Moon of a poem,

I promise I'll take astonishing pains to let the Moon be the Moon
the way pre-Watergate Republicans sincerely wanted Nixon
to be Nixon—although I would like fewer repercussions.
I swear I'll find the requisite strength to resist the ode, the idyll,

the insistent allegory, the threadbare costume drama of myth.
I vow absolutely to avoid, if I can, comparing its visual aspect
to anything more down-to-Earth—the last place we need to be going.
I guarantee that my Moon will never knowingly lend itself
to *symbol* or *metaphor* scrawled in the margins. It won't stand for
the heart, let's say. So if there's any waxing and waning to be done,
it will be only more or less the Moon. But for everyone's sake
I hope it doesn't come to any of that. Let's not worry about
what the Moon's up to when no one down here's looking.

## ii. My Uncle's Dilemma

I was a thoroughly unabashed child of the Space Race
growing up in the lovably erratic orbit of my uncle,
who uncovered budding conspiracies no matter where he went.
He brought every one of them home to live with him,
where they blossomed like crazy in his hothouse of a heart.
When it came to the Moon, he couldn't decide on his favorite:
the-Moon-we-never-really-landed-on but, rather, reconstructed
on a soundstage in the desert Southwest—although for all that
fuss and cinematographic bother, it might have been easier
just to actually *go*. Or the don't-be-an-idiot,
of-course-we-did Moon, but what we eventually discovered there—
after the golf, after a couple of Rover spins around the lunar block—
is the hushed-up reason why we haven't gone back since 1972:
a hostile race of beings that live beneath the cratered, rocky surface.
To his way of thinking, there was a lot to be said for both ideas.

To my uncle, who watched way too much pro wrestling on TV,
the bad blood between these rival *Apollo*-Moon-landing factions
smacked of bragging rights to the title of Lunar Conspiracy Champion.
He couldn't choose between Haystacks Calhoun and Gorilla Monsoon
on the night those two behemoths went toe to toe at last, swaggering
around the ring, wild-eyed, shamelessly mugging for the cameras.
He truly believed in both of them on their own antithetical terms,
their signature moves so unflinchingly outlandish
that he had to stand and cheer each one in his darkened living room.
As a student of these mostly predictable affairs, he was betting
there was no way this match could end in anything but a draw,
and that seemed more than fair, and fine by him, but
when Haystacks and Gorilla ganged up instead on the hapless referee,
they were hit with the one thing my uncle didn't see coming:
an incredible double-disqualification he'd never quite recover from—

as if he'd also been summarily disqualified for absolutely nothing
more than letting his emotions get the best of him as well
in a world where too few people are sufficiently moonstruck,
ever get carried away for no good reason, or any kind of reason,
they can think of. Much as we might wish it otherwise.

### iii. Final Offer

I've always tried taking what's left of the Moon
a little bit seriously, but at only a sixth of our usual gravity,
the Moon's almost never a solemn occasion. And I'm letting it go
for next to nothing here at the end. Poems can't seem to do business
any other way. By now it's already too late for you
to refuse a genuine deal like this—even if you're not about to forget
being promised nothing short of the Moon a few times before,
and it turned out more to resemble a long weekend in Omaha.

There's no chance of that happening now, at this historical moment
when you could indeed be reading the last Moon poem ever,
so maybe you should start the hard work of memorization.
Or else, when people come to you later and ask *How did it go?*
and *What was the Moon really like in those days?*
you might have to say *I don't remember much, but for some reason
there was wrestling.* And everyone will look up into the night
with its bright profusion of stars, but no Moon to speak of:
it's another new Moon phasing back into fashion, taking shape,
but just barely, in the sky. The next thing you know, here come
another thousand years when we're supposed to fawn all over it.

# III.

# Interlude: A Dozen from the Dream Chair

◦ ◦ ◦ ◦ ◦ ◦ ◦ ◦ ◦

*You are interested in the unknown, the mysterious, the unexplainable.*
*That is why you are here.*

　　—The Amazing Criswell, *Plan 9 from Outer Space*

*with gratitude for the living-room chair I fall asleep in*
*and the odd gifts it proffers from time to time—*
*provided I can actually decipher the scrawlings I've made*
*in the semi-conscious dark of the night before . . .*

# A Literary Fashion Statement

*for Ron*

When I sent a few new poems, none over fifteen lines, to my friend—
a forty-year veteran reader of my poems that, shall we say, don't often
settle down in the cozy confines of a single page, or even two—it was really
a desperate cry for help: *Please disabuse me of these. I can't keep them*
*from coming. They wake me up at night, and if that's not bad enough,*
*too many hang around for days, expecting me to entertain them, when surely*
*I have better things to do.*

                    And because they took so little time to read,
my friend wrote back immediately with his five-word declaration: *Short*
*is the new Long!* He made it sound like cause for celebration, but then
the dread came on. So now I hope he's only kidding, or he's wrong,
or else like anything in fashion for a while: this, too, shall pass.
*I'll bury this guy in the* old *Long again!* was my eventual response,
but it wasn't very long at all before I was surprisingly finished—
having come up short again, whether any of us liked it or not.

## One of the Roughs

*7 cents for a cup of coffee and 19 cents for a beefsteak—and me so fond of*
*coffee and beefsteak.*

> —Walt Whitman, in a letter to his brother from Boston, bemoaning
> his extravagance in restaurants (1860)

Hey: this here camerado's got
a lot more *Leaves of Grass* to go,
and there's no barbaric yawping, really,
after herbal tea and grapefruit.
So let's leave that kind of meal instead
to the likes of John Greenleaf Whittier.

## Fame Is Both Relative and Fleeting

We already know who's king
in the country of the blind,
but in the country of the deaf
a one-eyed king's unheard of.

# The Scientologist's Nightmare

Being charged by the minute, not by the mile
in the heavy traffic of everyday life,
and yes, the E-meter's running.

## Last-Ditch Prayer for the Lovers

Tonight's a dark river they're nowhere
near the end of. Behind them
all the bridges are on fire. There's no
sure boat, no kayak or canoe,
so let each of them be the other's raft
this one last time. Let them go
all the way down on each other.

## The Stress Is More Pronounced at Times, but It Is Always There

There are some days that seem so awfully long,
you're thinking *whiskey*. But you're thinking wrong.

There's no time to go soft. Instead, think strong
black coffee, a whole pot—its kickass song:
*Don't take the edge off, ever. Bring it on.*

Until your heartbeat's back where it belongs
to what's alive, still going on, not gone.

## When Did They Start Etching Reminders into the Side-View Mirrors on Cars?

*Objects are closer than they appear.*

Sadly, objects of your love and affection seldom are
closer than they appear. That would be more often true
of religious crackpots, tofu, an IRS audit,
and anyone you ever once were especially glad to think of
as, at best, a distant relative.

## Mysticism and American Politics

As soon as someone says *without a doubt*,
there's doubt. Without a doubt.

## Tonight's Feature: *Revenge of the Inside-Out, Multiple-Personalities Haiku*

*It Came From Beyond Grade School!!!*
Seventeen natures,
often about syllables.

## Why Plans 1 through 8 from Outer Space Came Undone— and Plan 9, Too, for That Matter

*for TJ—pro wrestling's "Swedish Angel" and Planet Earth's ace-in-the-hole, thanks to his friend Ed Wood's own, keener sense of planning and direction*

No Tor Johnson.
No Tor Johnson.
No Tor Johnson.
No Tor Johnson.
No Tor Johnson.
No Tor Johnson.
No Tor Johnson.
No Tor Johnson.

Way too much Tor Johnson.

# A Brief Guide to the Art of Give-and-Take with the World

Give the world your full consideration—
take it or leave it after that.
You can give thanks. You can take offense.
Give it to me. Take it back.
Give me a hard time. Take it easy.
Give it your best shot or take a rain-check.
Give birth or take a nap.
Give your own two cents. Take my advice.
Give it away. Take it to the bank.
Give it up or take it on the lam

just as long as you give a damn
for as long as you can take it.
Then take a breath
and try to give
a damn all over again.

## Posted at Charon's Bait & Tackle / Ferry Service

*NO SWEARING: YOU KNEW THIS DAY WOULD COME.*

*NO SPITTING.*

     *NO LOITERING.*

         *NO SWIMMING.*

*NO HALLOWEEN MASKS ALLOWED ON THESE PREMISES.*

*NO FLASH PICTURES.*

*PASSENGERS ONLY BEYOND THIS POINT.*

*NO RETURNS.*

     *NO EXCHANGES.*

         *NO REFUNDS.*

*PAYMENT REQUIRED AT TIME OF SERVICE.*

*WE RESERVE THE RIGHT TO REFUSE SERVICE TO ANYONE.*

*NO STANDING WHEN BOAT IS IN MOTION.*

*AND YES—WE HAVE FRESH NIGHTCRAWLERS.*

# IV.

# As Long as We Keep Going

∘ ∘ ∘ ∘ ∘ ∘ ∘ ∘ ∘

*We were overwhelming underdogs.*

—Yogi Berra

# Social Media and Me

*Alone: bad. Friend: good . . . friend good!*
> —Frankenstein's monster to the kindly hermit, *Bride of Frankenstein*
> (1935)

I don't like anything or anyone on Facebook. I neither make
nor take requests. I prefer real life, where actual friends
don't ask to be—or not since second grade, anyway.

Now, if only we were talking *anti*-social media,
it's possible I'd have a different attitude entirely.
Because there'd be no bastard sense of *friend* as active verb,
I could cut directly to the chase and go
on an *unfriending* rampage of historic proportions.
I'd be a more tenacious scourge than even Richard Nixon,
who was old-school relentless, keeping handwritten lists
of everyone he thought by any chance had done him wrong
in the slightest. It kept him going, living for the payback.

I'd go even further though, unfriending people I'd never
heard of before: anti-social master of the preemptive strike.
And I'd unfriend Richard Nixon, too—
even though he's more than twenty years in the grave—
just in case he's been using that down-time to dream up
another one of his unlikely, nearly supernatural comebacks.

Still, when it comes to the spiritless world of social media,
I've got to think that, if Richard Nixon were alive,
he wouldn't like anything or anyone on Facebook either.
That doesn't necessarily mean we'd actually be friends,
but we'd have something in common to talk about,

finally, beyond the bowling, how much we both like bowling.

I could also be so completely wrong, it isn't funny. Maybe
with a few drinks in him, he'd go friend-requesting crazy,
and when I'd say *Hey Nixon, how about some bowling,*
he'd say perhaps some other time,
he's a little busy right now—for the first time in forever
he's among friends. They've willingly accepted him
for who he is. They're way too young to know even half
of everything he was, and if that means good riddance at last
to Alger Hiss, rich-kid JFK, Vietnam, sabotaged peace talks,
Spiro Agnew, and Watergate, then what the hell's not to like?

But in the spirit of Nixon himself, I just can't seem to forget,
and if I've been reckless in giving him even this kind of life
that otherwise he might have deemed virtually impossible,
if accidentally I've created a huge social-media monster,
then I'll beg the same *full, free, and absolute pardon* he got,
deserving or not—right after he finally resigned, ducking out
on impeachment—from a sudden, well-meaning president
who'd already honestly tried to assure the rest of us once
and for all when he said *Our long national nightmare is over.*

# At the Convention of State Librarians, I Should Have Been Preaching to the Choir

*for John Furlong, who thought inviting me was a good idea*

They were so much less reserved than I'd expected
on that long-overdue weekend away from their workaday
library lives, hundreds come to convene in the raucous
fellowship of presentations, panels, breakout sessions followed
by cocktail-hour small talk and then dinner itself, which at last
is where I came in—Mr. Hopelessly Old-Fashioned Keynote Speaker
who'd driven himself dizzy all afternoon in room after room
of dealers and their can't-live-without products for "Your 21st-Century
Library": uploads and downloads, hard drives, software, plug-ins,
e-readers, flash drives, iThis and iThat, and memory beyond any
mortal understanding. I was killing time, hoping to check out displays
of actual books, or at least some whispered suggestion of books.
I kept saying *just browsing*. They suggested Firefox or Chrome
until I gave up and bought a pair of good-wood newspaper sticks
from the one guy with nothing electronic to offer.

I draped them with sections of *The Kansas City Star*
and brought them with me to the podium, righteously insisting
on flying the flag of some all-but-forgotten country of words on paper
during "My Hometown Library," in which I spoke of one extremely
gracious librarian who went out of her way repeatedly
to guide a fledgling explorer discovering a plenitude of books
when there wasn't a website anywhere in the world to navigate
and my only operating system was courtesy of Melvil Dewey,
whose decimal precision let me know specifically how much reading
there was to be done in this life.

The librarians of Missouri
couldn't wait for me to finish. Sooner than I'd planned on—
before I burst into pencil and paper and typewriter rhapsodies—
I sat down, the entire banquet hall at once as silent
as a library after hours, or even worse: boarded up and gone.

That night after falling asleep over *The Star* in my hotel bed,
I dreamed up the Royal Library at Alexandria before it burned—
its lecture halls, gardens, shrines for every one of the Nine Muses—
the single greatest archive in the knowable ancient world
where one hundred scholars lived full time to read and write,
translate and copy. Where *scroll* was the most reliable of nouns,
not some whimsical up-and-down verb. I dreamed back even farther
to the library at Ur, where Amit Anu was known as "Tablet Keeper"—
effectively, the first librarian ever—where *tablet* meant knowledge
forever set in stone. Even if those libraries somehow had survived,
surely these days they'd be mostly staffed with IT people.

And in my last dream of the evening, Bertha Skevington—
my not-so-gracious hometown librarian nemesis—sat down on my bed,
her 1962 scowl now perfectly immortal. For the first time ever
I was glad to see her peering over my shoulder. She'd heard me
talking in my sleep, and out of primordial third-grade force of habit
I said it wasn't me whispering to Debbie Fuller what I was cribbing
word for word from the *World Book Encyclopedia* this time:
*Ecuador exports foodstuffs*—good enough for me, although even now
I'm still not positive what foodstuffs are. Sometimes Bertha called
the police station a block away, and sometimes a cop would show up
just to calm her down, to restore her precarious sense of order.
And whenever she went into her *In case you hadn't noticed,*
*we're surrounded here by books* routine, there would be no escaping
her inevitable crying. She truly did love books, the very idea

of books, as much as she hated kids. And we were far too young
to know any better, always one homework assignment behind.

But in the dream she told me that things were completely different now,
that it was my mortal duty to raise my voice, to talk up books
before it was too late, that I'd given up way too easily at dinner.
This historic occasion wasn't lost on me: Bertha Skevington
and I, for once, were finally on the same unlikely page.

In the morning the librarians were gathered at breakfast,
hung over but nonetheless comparing electronic notes when I stood up
renewed, unannounced, in the middle of the scrambled eggs,
for what I still believed in—the *World Book*, 1962, and Debbie Fuller—
exclaiming one more fact I was absolutely sure of: *And Bolivia
exports tin!* over and over, even as the sleepy security guard
escorted me out of the hall. It was so quiet in there again
that for a moment they seemed nearly like genuine librarians
who knew their long weekend was just about mercifully over,
and when I looked back over my shoulder, I could have sworn
I saw Bertha Skevington almost smiling and waving
an unmistakable book in the air while the 21st-Century librarians
finished their breakfast in peace, looking so unreasonably happy
to be left here at the end, without a doubt, to their own devices.

## In Newton's Time, When Physics Was Physics, They Partied Till Dawn or They Didn't Party at All, but Today's Physics Wants to Have It Both Ways

Maxwell's shown up with his Demon in tow.
Schrodinger's schlepped his sweet Cat—
though depending on which of two rooms you peek into,
you might not quite see it as That.

Heisenberg, never too sure of himself,
has steered clear of the ladies all night,
while Feynman comes on with his bongos, of course,
and as usual that guy does all right.

The annoying Nikola Tesla for once
left his coil and his pigeons at home.
Still, no one's real sorry when Hawking wheels through
and knocks Tesla clean out of this poem.

All things being equal—at least Energy
and Mass times the Speed of Light squared—
you can tell Einstein's had the space-time of his life
just by getting a load of his hair.

Sir Isaac looks down on this particle science
from the height of his outmoded heaven
and says, of those partying bodies in motion,
*They'll be bodies at rest by 11.*

And the tighter they get, the looser the talk:
party physics in action. Don't panic
unless there's no old-fashioned wrench to be found
in this house full of quantum mechanics.

## There Will Be a Test on This—or on Something Else Entirely

**i.**

So much information is junk information—
it's nothing we would have gone out of our way for,
but now that we have it, we don't understand
why it feels like something we've known all along.

And then there's the matter of misinformation—
not knowing it's wrong information passed on.
Misguided on purpose, it's *dis*information,
made up to achieve some mischievous end:

to topple a government, bankrupt a business,
undo a marriage or medical practice.
It serves as distraction, diverting attention
from whatever we might be even right now

this damn close to knowing, according to those
who know more than we, the hard facts we're better
off never quite knowing, so maybe we'd best
stick to what seems like well-worn information.

Remember what happens, and not just in movies,
to people who know what's considered too much.
They're silenced forever, asleep with the fishes
or vanished in thin air around the next corner.

## ii.

Let's touch on a few things that won't be much trouble
as long as you don't wait too long to get going:

places-to-catch-bigger-fish information,
radio-telescope-dish information,
make-a-killer-potato-knish information,
there's-no-way-that-Shakespeare-wrote-*this* information,
people-who've-never-been-kissed information,
temptations-too-hard-to-resist information,
how-to-schedule-your-own-secret-tryst information,
extremely-rare-Franz-Joseph-Liszt information,
the dreaded we-really-insist information,
the-court-dates-you'd-better-not-miss information
along with some cease-and-desist information,
worries-you-shouldn't-dismiss information,
so-blow-out-the-candles-and-wish information
and, finally, cross-this-off-your-list information.

Mostly we know too much or too little,
and no one knows categorically what we're in for.
That's dangerous either way and, as usual,
tomorrow's bound to be its own confounding test—
with any luck, maybe short-answer for once.

# Sonata for Tornado in EF-5 (Major): May 22, 2011, 5:41–6:13 p.m.

*The people of Joplin were going about their daily lives on a Sunday evening: cooking supper, watching TV, walking the dog. And then came the whirlwind, nearly a mile wide and six miles long.*
  —Missouri Governor Jay Nixon

*It was more like walking through* The Twilight Zone *than walking down Main Street.*
  —resident Eddie Atwood, the day after

*for the citizens of Joplin—the dead and the living—victims and survivors of the single deadliest U.S. tornado in 62 years of record-keeping history*

**i.**

There's no one anywhere in town who's worried about much
of anything on a breezy Sunday afternoon like this:
Little League baseball in the park or a high school graduation
or firing up the barbeque under a sky that's seemed so unreasonably
clear all day, and even a last-minute run to the Gas-N-Go
for cigarettes, sunglasses, one more cold six-pack just in case
is truly no problem at all, even though the guy behind the counter
won't stop talking about his to-die-for Saturday night, even now
as he's getting louder, raising his voice so he can be heard
over the rising noise of sirens going off as so often they do
out of nowhere, here on the eastern edge of Tornado Alley, so yes,
he hears them but no, not really, because the truth is: tornadoes
have touched down hard only twice in the last forty years of sirens
just like these. But this particular day's about to turn on everyone
unthinkably fast, although they can't quite see it that way yet.

If a *watch* means conditions that could easily lend themselves
to genuine, impending trouble, then most of us have carried on—
weather and geography aside—under one kind of watch or another
in effect for our whole lives. When that turns into an audible *warning*
about whatever could be headed our way, in theory there should be
at least a little time to prepare for the worst. But the fact is
it's never sufficient. With hurricanes, there might be entire days
to know each one by name, and still too many people remain
unmoved. They end up stuck in the eye of the storm. With tornadoes?
At best, twenty minutes—and that's with radar and subsequent sirens.

This is where folks are right now, I'm afraid—the headlong rush
to hunker down, the trying to lie low. And blankets and pillows too,
if they're handy. Forget about those solitary nights they didn't do
nearly enough good. This time it's not about looking for comfort,
but instead—in all likelihood—unmetaphorical, tangible flying debris.

## ii.

They're standing five-deep in the dark of the Gas-N-Go's walk-in cooler,
and what happens next is anyone's guess in a world this awfully small,
reduced to nothing but soundtrack—a continuous deep rumbling,
locomotive or jet engine or thundering waterfall, depending on
who's trying to put such a primal sound into words—a crazy-strong
200-mile-an-hour wind that's barely an outside-world away.
Not to mention the excruciating pressure.

                                   It's best they can't see
what's exploding off the shelves on the other side of the cooler door
straining its hinges but hanging on, this near to bursting wide open:
breath mints, magazines, candy bars, a flying wedge of Little Debbie
no-expiration snack cakes. They can't see the façade of the Gas-N-Go
breaking completely apart, going and suddenly gone. Can't see
the power lines down, twitching out sparks that will light up the gas

spewing from broken mains, homes and buildings on fire for miles.
And they can't see how much of this city is currently up in the air:
street signs, trash cans, windowpanes. WELCOME mats and floorboards.
Whole families unceremoniously blown out of their living rooms.

In the cooler they're actually sweating it out, praying and crying
and holding one another, wondering why these few minutes seem more
than even an overblown lifetime. Someone's humming *Nearer, My God,
to Thee*. Someone's singing *Over the Rainbow*. And that radio preacher
who'd wrongly predicted the end of the world for last night—what if
he'd somehow come closer than anyone thought just this morning?
A guy with no time for the Rapture swears to hell with Harold Camping,

what matters is right here and now—a second disconcerting round of hail.
The ten-year-old kid, who's already had quite a day at shortstop,
who's also unabashedly something of a fifth-grade weather geek,
says hail forms at a tornado's leading edge, then once more in its wake.
They can't be sure he really knows what he knows, but they have seen
this kid's arm from deep in the hole, his unerring long throw to first.
They're afraid to say a word. They're holding what's left of their breath
in the dark and, with luck, in the ever-widening, elemental quiet.

## iii.

It's surely nothing less than a flat-out, windblown wonder
that anyone's left standing after the furious spinning winds down,
after the attendant howling mostly has subsided. And yet here
they come, those people stunned but slowly emerging from coolers,
from low-lying ditches, from the legendary southwest corner
of basements—some still dragging behind them the last-minute blankets
they found extra refuge in. Now it's these tentative baby steps, as if
for once, knee-deep in their lives, they truly have to start over,
making their separate ways back into a clearly more harrowing world.

They knew the drill, and they know this aftermath-part-of-it too:
the deep breathing in, then the gradual exhalation. Soon they'll be giving
themselves the once-over, searching for cuts and abrasions. The bruises
won't show up until later. There will be some who would rather not look
at the devastation behind them—in any direction they're headed,
not even a hundred yards from the end of someone else's world—but
they'll find themselves staring all the same. In debris nearly three feet deep:
torn-open animals minus their stuffing, a Darth Vader Halloween mask,
a birdcage, snapshots of birthdays and weddings, *Let It Bleed* and *Let It Be*
CDs, statues of St. Christopher in a jumble of steering wheels, a crucifix
driven into the trunk of the only tree holding its ground, and a smaller
unlikely miracle—a perfectly untangled Slinky coiled tight at the top
of a flight of stairs heading nowhere.

                        And as for the citizens alive tonight
in a city they can scarcely identify: everyone's a stroke-of-luck survivor
on the move, however slow their progress, looking out for the others.

## iv.

This is about the need to make sense
of what never will make sense, but still:
this is about the trying. This is not
about a return to normal. Although
the pressure has fallen to its more
natural level, there is always pressure.
In that way it's a lot like gravity.

This is by no means a metaphor—
not after 161 dead. The wind
has only died *down*. Not *out*.
There will always be wind. This is not
some allegorical *picking up the pieces*.
This means to gather what's hopelessly

broken on the ground—detritus
to sigh over, maybe, when salvage isn't
possible. This means getting on with it
as more than a figure of speech,
proceeding one arduous step at a time,
making discernible strides.

                    You can see
it's not exactly easy to negotiate
a realm this insistently literal.
But it's time to make something new
out of all this water and mud and
wind-swept straw, something notably
solid—not *like* a brick, but the brick
itself. Then another on top of that one,
the way the ancients built dwellings
and temples and tombs. We know this
because these things now and then
weathered the stormy forces of history—
so much of that broken beauty still
surviving, still undeniably here
in this world without end yet. Amen.

# Man Ray Stares into the Future of Jazz

*after his tempera and ink aerograph,* Jazz *(1919)*

Picture a quartet on the bandstand, drawn into
the colors of pure sound:
a whisper across a wet reed,
the age-old tension between drum and stick,
fingers just now touching down on the bass strings
and the keyboard, and maybe the Moon, for all anyone knows
about this history on the edge of being made.
Someone's looking inside those black and white notes rising,
breaking free of their staves, swirling and jumping
and curling, coming back together in wave after wave—
towering sheets of music sure to turn the shape of jazz

inside out. And whoever listens to it will be utterly unstrung,
assuredly giddy in this unheard-of spectrum,
and whatever they'd planned on doing for the rest of the day
will have to wait. They'd rather improvise instead, like mad,
all over the place. Later there will be time for Miles and Trane,
the Duke and the Count, Prez and Monk and Dizzy and Bird—
all the colorful names of jazz still to come—

but right now it's this offbeat cat Man Ray, from Philly
and, man, he's laying it down in those crazy, tinted shades
of gone yellow, gone orange, gone blue and green, and a few
there are no proper names for yet. He's blowing a cool breeze
of tempera and ink. He's stretching out, taking his solo
anywhere he likes the sound of. Clearly, he's seen
where the music is headed. He's heard something, and he's going
exquisitely on record, making a brilliant note of it.

# Trying on Hats with Rahsaan Roland Kirk

*(Madison, Wisconsin—February 1975)*

> *When I'm reincarnated, I'm gonna come back as a musical note.*
> —Rahsaan

### i.

I was working the hat-shop counter when he sauntered up
and asked, in all sincerity, *Do these hats make me look scary?*
and I wasn't sure if that was the look he was going for
or wanted, instead, to stay away from. With his gigantic smile,
dark wraparound glasses, and a pair of whistles around his neck,
he'd been living most of his life by feel since the age of two,
when he was blinded by bad medicine. So one by one
he held them in his hands and tried them on, improvising
his off-and-running, free-association commentary:

Full-blown Fedora: *This 1940s gumshoe always knows who done it.*
Stetson Western: *Yippee-i-ay! I'm Ben Cartwright's black-sheep son!*
Bowler: *Not bad, maybe, if the British are coming. Do you think the British*
  *are coming?*
Fez: *I'd have to boost me one of those tiny Shriner cars.*
Porkpie: *This should be worn only by the ghost of Lester Young.*
Beret: *Too old-hat-artiste these days for the more hip likes of me.*
And when he reached for the tam-o'-shanter, I thought

okay, *here* comes your scary, your ridiculous-pom-pom-scary—
but, truth is, somehow he looked good in everything, asking
*Where's the mirror?* over and over, pirouetting, carried away
in his own deep, melodious laughing. Finally he decided on

a jaunty leather Newsboy number: *The absolute extra, extra,*
*read-all-about-it best—and don't you bother with a bag.*
*I'm wearin' it to go.*

            I told him what an unexpected pleasure,
that I'd be in his audience that night, as it happened. *See you later,*
*Mr. Kirk* is what I must have said.

                   *Not if I see you first, kid, but please*
*do not hold your sweet white breath for that! And since you knew exactly*
*who I was, now kindly know me by* Rahsaan.

               Then he took his leave,
leaning on a walking-stick embellished with a mayhem of baubles.

## ii.

Onstage he was armed to the teeth with his trio of saxophones,
along with flutes, whistles, and bells at the ready, his legendary breath
powering every one of them through his personal universe
of nothing less than Black Classical Music. It was all the Gospel
according to Rahsaan and his fellow Vibration Society travelers:
New Orleans, hard bop, post-bop, soul, Black pop steeped
in shades of blue, his monumental breath blowing down the senseless
walls built up between them, his nonstop breath unleashing
two or three melodies at once, and in the same breath harmonizing
perfectly with each. Now *that* was scary, incomprehensible-scary.
And don't even get him started on the gong.

But when he threw those folding-chairs off the bandstand
in the general direction of some loud table-talk, people
oblivious to their own storied history in this music—
okay, finally, he looked just a little plain scary:
*You've got to get with the music or get out. You either swing*
*or split.* And as for those who wisely chose to stay,
Rahsaan swung us hard through everything he had,

delivering the news we didn't know we needed, news
that would never be the same news twice, to hear him tell it,
then bending over to whisper in my front-row, how-the-hell-
did-he-know ear: *Sorry, kid, but I'm afraid I can't quite*
*get away with this hat—it brings out my Inner Scary.*
*You wear it in good health for me and everyone, including you,*
*in the Vibration Society.*
                              And just like that, the set was over,
the lights came up, and I was out the door, getting away
with Rahsaan's hat, neither scared nor scary in the cold Wisconsin night.

### iii.

Later that year, a stroke shut down half of his body,
so he reconfigured his instruments, taught himself how
to coax the music out one-handed—some wicked-scary
love and dedication. Two years after that, a second stroke
took him entirely, literally out of this world at last, although
if he had anything to say about it, his dying breath just might have
been the start of some undying song he'd always known
his mortal body would turn into, transposing one note at a time,
if that's how it had to be—thousands of bright Rahsaan moments
lighting up the dark until all of us can see for ourselves again
and again there's almost nothing to be scared of, not as long
as there's music like this, and not as long as we are here
to get with that music and swing.

# My One-Performance-Only Dream: Night of the Jazz Giants' Shoes

*You can play a shoestring if you're sincere.*
　　　　—John Coltrane

*Good evening, my hip cats and with-it kitties. Before we dig*
*the holy sounds this group is fixing to lay down, please join me*
*in a most rousing, carousing, and foot-stomping welcome for*
*Mr. Charlie Parker, standing tall in the classy saddles,*
*soloing on "Scrapple from the Shoestring";*
*Mr. Dizzy Gillespie to-the-nines in the snappy alligators,*
*soloing on "A Shoestring in Tunisia";*
*Mr. Thelonious Monk in the nutty rhythm-a-ning tap shoes,*
*soloing on "Straight, No Shoestring";*
*Mr. Miles Davis in the two-tone wingtip oxfords,*
*soloing on "My Shoestring Valentine";*
*Mr. Charles Mingus in the steel-toed shit-kickers,*
*soloing on "Better Git It in Your Shoestring";*
*Mr. Sonny Rollins in the way-out-West moccasins,*
*soloing on "Sonnymoon for Shoestrings";*
*and to count it off for all of us: tonight's fearless leader,*
*Mr. John Coltrane in the Converse All Star high-tops, red,*
*soloing on "Giant Shoestrings" and "My Favorite Shoestrings."*
*I'm your most hip and royal host, Lord Buckley in bowling shoes,*
*soloing whenever I can on anything that rolls and smokes.*

And that's when I got bounced out of my own dream club.
I was deliriously close to hearing I-don't-know-what,
but even without the instruments that had taken them so far,
they could still be making some sincerely really crazy joyful noise.

## Listening to Some Kind of Bird

The sun was barely up, and I am hardly
ever in any condition to say those particular words,
yet there I was this morning, up and actually walking
past mourning doves already davening on the power line,
jays beside themselves in their compulsive squawking,
dark crow-shadows cawing, back from West Nile decimation,
and from out of nowhere, briefly, some birdsong more
ethereal, so downright tuneful I could tell straightaway
that even if I saw this lyric bird, I'd still have no idea

what it was, as what I know, ornithologically speaking,
wouldn't fill my empty morning coffee cup, unlike
those people who travel the far-flung world just to see
and record their hard-won sightings of so many birds
I've never heard or heard of, adding more colorful names
to their *I-Love-Birding* master-lists, because those nutty
*birders* are nothing if not a meticulous, dedicated bunch,

although today it was only me a few blocks from home,
nothing if not ludicrous among these early birds, my heart
full of The Stray Birds' *Dream in Blue*—still more birds
I didn't know until a true friend played their song for me—
and it wasn't long before I thought I heard every one of
my neighborhood birds singing that blue song too, and
why shouldn't they, being stray birds themselves, get in
on this blue morning's action, because while I'm not liable
to stray nearly far enough in my lifetime to see, say, even

half of the world's more-than-ten-thousand species of birds,
it dawned on me that I can more than hold my own

when it comes to blue in so many of its shades, that I know blue
like nobody's blue business, can discern its telltale plumage
in the most unlikely places, detect a single feather's-worth
of blue from an astonishing distance because I've gone to
great lengths, spared no emotional expense, repeatedly stood
in harm's way just to listen to another of its siren-songs, some days
low-down, some days positively soaring, like that kind of blue
Miles laid down with his midnight horn—not quite sad, not
really, more like pensive, oddly commodious, as if that late-night
feeling could come over anyone, even in broad daylight—

which for no good reason is what today's been mostly like
all day, and maybe later I can add it to my own master-list
of every day I didn't come undone completely, not as long
as I kept singing whatever words came out, loud, the way
my neighbor couldn't help his booming *It's a beautiful day*,
referring, I'm sure, to the cool breeze, the blue of morning sky
without a single cloud, although I think a few clouds always
bring out a deeper blue myself, the blue beneath the blue,

and by then my heart was perilously close to bursting
into its very own audacious stray-bird song, composed
of everything that already had occurred to me this morning,
but that wouldn't be what my neighbor had in mind, so
instead I gave it to him short, I gave it to him sweet and easy,
in what I hoped might pass for music to his ears: *It sure is*, and
it truly was, the way I heard it, the way I saw it too.

# Between the '60s and the Saucers and the Willy-Nilly Gods—Let Alone the Vagaries of Ordinary Mortals—It's Hard to Know Who Needs Believing Most

## i. All He Knew to Say

*Saw a flying saucer at State Junction 6 and 63. Believe it or not.*
> —Ashland, Nebraska patrolman Herbert Schirmer's log-out entry
> for December 3, 1967 (3:00 a.m.)

Because he was twenty-two years old, naturally he thought he knew
everything, had already seen whatever there was to see,
and near the end of his shift, 2:20 a.m., it was just his luck
that the blinking red lights of a disabled truck at the roadside
would mean a slightly longer night than he was looking for.
But in his cruiser's high-beams was something else completely:
a metallic craft with illuminated portholes and some kind of crazy
catwalk around it, hovering soundlessly a few feet off the ground.
He watched it slowly rising in the crisp Nebraska air, passing
directly over his car, lighting up the sky before it disappeared
like just another shot in the dark.

                                Back at the station to log out
before heading home, where he'd try hard to close his wide-open eyes,
he discovered that his routine, ten-minute final swing through town
had taken an extra half-hour. He wrote down his fourteen words
to prove he wasn't quite speechless. Because he was an officer of the law,
he knew by heart the Miranda right-to-remain-silent bit, but he was also
twenty-two, and no way on Earth would he leave it at that for long—
believe the-rest-of-what-happened-or-not-out-there. Or not.

## ii. A Little Too Quick to Respond

> *Are you the watchman of this place?*
>
> —alien's first words to Schirmer, part of the lost half-hour
> "recovered" during hypnosis sessions in 1968

And because he was a twenty-two-year-old officer of the law, he simply answered
*Sure* without asking any questions of his own, such as what
they could possibly mean by *this place*, more or less, if anything at all
beyond this immediate intersection of small-town country roads. Probably
he wasn't thinking even as big as Ashland, let alone Nebraska or the rest
of the unsuspecting country—and especially not the whole precariously
lightheaded planet, where suddenly they found themselves at that odd
interrogative moment spinning into the slippery junction of 1967 and 1968.
And what is a watchman supposed to do, specifically, in such a situation?
It's a thankless job, so surely anyone would be grateful
for a freshly starched uniform, name tag, working two-way radio,
hot coffee, and maybe some semblance of a gun, no matter how underloaded.

And before Schirmer's aliens actually arrived—when they were still traveling
mightily through stretches of empty interstellar space, only to wind up,
for all their cosmic know-how, in ASHLAND, NEBRASKA: POP. *2000—*
there was so much genuine commotion already in the 1967 air
that watchman Herbert Schirmer couldn't see any cause for alarm:

### iii. Disturbances in the 1967 Space-Time Continuum

B-movie Republican Reagan is sworn in as California's governor
one day before the Doors let loose with *Light My Fire*, and without even trying,
there will be many days for swearing in and nights to set on fire this year.

In NASA's burning hurry to the Moon, the harried crew of *Apollo 1* goes up
in launchpad flames three weeks away from liftoff. Sealed in for numbing hours
of routine system-checks, they were looking for trouble. But they never asked for any
so suddenly enormous that they couldn't get out of it somehow alive.
And in the name of U.S. rocket science, it's back to the Space Race drawing board.

Over San Francisco's Golden Gate Park, the Moon's so much closer
and more peaceful to the Human Be-In throng, where alternative-wavelength DJs
Ginsberg and Leary exhort thousands of un-Republicans to *Turn on,*
*tune in, drop out.* It's a countdown to anti-ignition, a send-up in smoke
of the cartoon American Dream, the ultimate warm-up act for the tenuous

Summer of Love ahead, complete with tourists bus-tripping through the Haight
to *See Real-Life Hippies!* That's what small-time Charlie Manson—
just released from jail again—is doing, armed with a guitar, his ingratiating
smile, and dreams about a family he'd one day more than own up to.
Hendrix is setting fire to another Stratocaster down in Monterey,

and it's a different kind of scorcher altogether, this Summer of anti-Love
in Newark, Cleveland, Memphis, Detroit: fires there'll be no putting out completely.
When heavyweight Ali says *No* to the Army, *No* to the war in Vietnam, and
*I'm so pretty* to anyone who'll listen, he's stripped of the crown he otherwise wasn't
about to lose, and once more the country is torn between sheer outrage
and outright inflammatory cheering. And this stubborn split-decision fever

isn't breaking anytime soon: it's the big-screen year of *Cool Hand Luke*—or the year
of *Bonnie and Clyde.* Either Elvis, singing his still viable heart out on *How Great*
*Thou Art*—or the Beatles, *getting by with a little help from* their *friends.*
Consider the Patterson Bigfoot film just in from Bluff Creek, California:

when that creature slows down to look directly back at the camera,
it's proof of an unabashed animal's native curiosity—or
a man in a costume who's checking to see if Patterson's still shooting.

In the same discombobulated October week of the off-Broadway
dawning of *Hair*, with its promise of New Age relief on the way, astrologically
speaking—*Aquarius* ad nauseam—reaction to the escalating war
is heating up here at home: recruiters from Dow Chemical on campus
in Madison, Wisconsin—selling in so many words the future of napalm—
are confronted by hundreds of infuriated students. When police arrive
in their otherworldly riot gear, it's obvious that no one's had any kind
of time to prepare for this outrageous midterm exam.

A thousand miles away, 100,000 protestors gather at the Lincoln Memorial—
the first-ever national anti-war demonstration. Some in that crowd
can't wait to attempt the decidedly radical, non-metaphorical
*levitation of the Pentagon itself*—one handbill's madcap call-to-arms—
by chanting or singing or telekinesis or whatever passes these days for prayer.
Or even some literal heavy lifting, if that's what finally has to be done
*to exorcize the evil spirits of war.* To let the sun shine in.
But the Pentagon winds up so easily holding its shadowy, dark ground.

And on the same day the saucer arrives at last and begins its descent
in the middle of watchman Schirmer's particular nowhere—yet another
unfortunate *they-never-land-on-the-White-House-lawn* situation—
the first human heart is successfully transplanted half a world away,
and finally there's a little good news this late in what's been one
exceedingly strenuous year. This heartsick planet surely could use

some kind of lift about now, so let it be this groundbreaking surgery, or
a message of hope from alien beings who've gone so far out of their way again
to deliver it—if that's what it turns out they're here for.
In either case, may there be a few auspicious days on the bright side
before the complications unavoidably set in: the body, threatening

to reject the new heart it sorely needs, or the brain so close to shutting down,
unwilling to graciously entertain the idea of such unexpected visitors.

The heart patient won't make it to Christmas, and Schirmer's in no position yet
to get the celestial message. It will be next year before he remembers too much
of anything that's happened. And whether those intrepid aliens in fact
hurtled through so many light-years to reach us
or wormholed their way to our planet instead in no time at all,
it's hard to believe they're already leaving, almost as if
they were never really here, saving their very best advice for last:

## iv. Running Down the Gods

*We want you to believe in us—but not too much.*
—alien's final words to Schirmer, "recovered" in 1968

What a welcome change of pace on the part of assuredly superior beings
who must have known they wouldn't always be there for Herbert Schirmer
or anyone else, for that matter. Because too often the faithful, whatever the faith,
believe until it hurts. Just think of the demanding Old Testament God, or
the Wizard of Oz, if you must. They're working behind the scenes
in their respective jurisdictions, bent over improvised control boards—
pushing this, pulling that, frantically turning some other thing—
and throwing their weighty voices around. Go ask Abraham and Isaac, or Job
and his fed-up wife. Or Lot's wife: for looking back over her shoulder toward home,
she was summarily iodized. At least the Wizard said he'd settle for a broom,
never honestly believing that Dorothy could deliver, and what else can he do
but sputter and play for a little more time? Those wayward Greek and Roman gods
weren't any better—capricious, petty, quick to anger at any slight, real
or imagined—famously insisting on blind faith in their unruly powers.

And down here at the mortal level, it only gets worse: people with too much
faith in themselves, always asking much the same of others—their excessive trust
and understanding, yes, and even more distressingly, undying admiration.
It's a patchwork of abstracted virtue sure to wear thin in this era of too many
prime ministers and presidents, attorneys and investment bankers, military
officers and corporate CEOs, preachers and physicians, artists and writers
and radio talk-show hosts and TV weather-people who expect us to believe
they can predict, a full week in advance, the daily highs and lows we're in for.

## v. Too Much 1968

No one could have forecast 1968, an unrivalled year of too much
believing, bleeding, and dying. And no nightwatchman anywhere on patrol
could so much as hope to slow its approach, so here it comes:

Walter Cronkite will return from reporting on Vietnam's deadly Tet Offensive
to his anchor desk at CBS News, where this *Most Trusted Man in America*
stymies the Johnson administration by pronouncing the war unwinnable.
Then the massacre at My Lai, although details of those three lost hours
won't be uncovered for another year: Lieutenant Calley's *I was just following
orders*, his men in turn following his, and 500 women and children wiped out
for no military reason. When war-torn LBJ goes on television to announce
there's no way he'll run again, Martin Luther King can't believe what he's seeing,

can't help his out-loud *Amen*. It's a week before he'll go down himself, for good,
on a Memphis motel balcony, and soon enough hard-running Democrat
Bobby Kennedy too, on a restaurant-kitchen floor in Ronald Reagan's California—
too much and too much—and people who'd put their faith in them will try again
to sift through the sadness and anger for anything still left standing
if the cities ever stop burning again. And there might not be much.
Surely it can't be Richard Nixon—inexplicably back from the dead

and calling himself *The New Nixon* until it's all a bit much, tricked out
with those morally ambiguous *Nixon's the One* bumper stickers—yet somehow
his *Peace with Honor* campaign catches fire at Miami's Republican Convention.
Chicago's Mayor Daley unofficially will host the bloody Democratic Convention,
offering his own butchered peacemaker's pledge: *The policeman's not there
to create disorder; the policeman's there to preserve disorder.* And stumbling
out of this confusion will be Hubert Humphrey, too much the LBJ lap dog
to start pissing with the big dogs now. And believe it or not, it's Nixon
promising, if elected, to end the war. He'll keep referring to his *secret plan*
like something cooked up after spending too much time with Spanky and Alfalfa
in the *Little Rascals* clubhouse. But Nixon in the White House is a different story.
His new rough-and-tumble gang's hijinks will be no laughing matter.

Before the year's gone, Charles Manson also will remake himself with a vengeance—
more of a Family man than ever. He'll pass long days in his homemade bunker
working up his own much-too-secret plan to launch a new, helter-skelter war.
He'll listen too much to the *White Album*, finding messages he truly believes
were intended for him alone, already dreaming his way down the road
to his wild-eyed historical moment—a bare-bones production of Armageddon
and Bethlehem together, live in concert, high in the fabled Los Angeles hills.

The year cinematically ushered in by Kubrick's expansive, luminous *2001*
will go out with the *Apollo 8* astronauts' more immediate space odyssey:
clearing a flight-path for 1969, the much ballyhooed Moon landing still ahead.
They'll take that lucky-shot "Earthrise" photo from lunar orbit—instantly
a Christmas-card classic presenting a beautiful, overwrought planet
in this far-more-flattering-than-usual light. Peace on Earth, then, as if
that could happen. And with honor, whatever that means. Back here at the movies,

a world away from the Moon's breathtaking heights, this year will finally trail off
in low-budget black and white: Romero's claustrophobic, unrelenting *Night
of the Living Dead*. And after the lights come on again
it will be a new year where, when it comes to steering clear of zombies
or the landlord or even Richard Nixon in the flesh or in theory, at last
we might like our chances—if that's not, just this once, too much to ask.

## vi. What Comes Back

*We've been watching the human race for a long time,* the space beings say
in too many preachy 1950s science fiction movies and in those slaphappy
pamphlets and books by people who'd trafficked, however briefly, with real-life
Space Brothers and Sisters. With apostolic fervor, they were forever talking up
the unearthly wisdom first imparted just to them—most often, oddly bland
concerns and admonitions about Earth's new Atomic Age. But at least
in those glory days of flying saucers, before the darker UFO abduction ruckus—
forbidding Greys, invasive implants, human/alien hybrid babies on display—
a person could simply walk right onto a spaceship and straightaway get taken
for a ride: an exclusive, invitation-only adventure. And every one of them
remembered it completely, not a single minute mysteriously gone missing.
No hypnosis required. The experience was all theirs, anytime they wanted,
and always their decidedly unmitigated pleasure to relive.

Herbert Schirmer's close encounter split the historical difference. Apparently
he'd held up his end of the wee-hours conversation, small-talking his way
inside the craft. But that was nowhere in his waking recollection.
He used to listen time and again to recordings where the aliens themselves,
unmenacing, came back to him in lengthy hypnotic regressions. Even then
he never quite got off the ground before everyone had somewhere else to be.
They made him a high-flown promise they'd return—*Watchman, one day
you'll see the universe!*—and although he believed they might have had
nothing but mostly good intentions, he didn't get far when it came to thinking
it could really happen. That would have meant a little too much
hoping against hope—more than he could hold out for the rest of his life.
As if he'd ever have that luxury, that kind of time again.

## vii. Where the Rest of Us Get Off

And when it comes to where the rest of us on Earth put our faith,
history tells us repeatedly that we have to watch ourselves.
We'd never knowingly get onboard with a bad idea, but it appears
that's more than occasionally where we've been, right in the middle of
the wrong crowd again, and any lost time we can't account for later
gets a little harder to make up. We really don't remember being told
in no uncertain terms what to believe—let alone what for, and
how wholeheartedly—by someone plainly asking so many for so much.
The next time we get that carried away, let's try not giving up too much
for no good reason.

                     In earlier, more optimistic days, we shook hands
on anything. Freely gave our solemn word. Made what we considered
sacrifices. Sizable donations. We signed petitions, paid most of our taxes,
and shook our heads when we got wise to another war we'd been sold.
We bought smaller cars and still recalled next to nothing when we woke up
to find ourselves as usual out of gas, muttering in the breakdown lane again
with no idea how we got there. We'd only wanted to go home.

This could be our final good-faith offer, when enough at last will have to be
enough. Then we make our move toward the door, where we get off
saying take it or leave it, no questions asked, believe it
or not, before heading back to anywhere we might have come from once—
palatial estate or cold-water flat, lover or leftover casserole, long-ago
hometown or faraway-planet-of-the-so-inclined—somewhere almost
always beyond belief from here. Back to those lives we've led ourselves
to believe in just enough: that as long as we keep going, we're not gone.

# V.
# Epilogue

o o o o o o o o o

*Too late to stop now.*

　　—Van Morrison, *Into the Mystic*

# Study Guide

What is the poet so desperately trying to say?
Do you honestly think it's something worth hearing?
How would you characterize his tone—
monotonous, dodgy, or unusually willy-nilly?
Are you already wishing for more personification?
More allusion? More metaphors? More *anything*?
Is his subject matter worthy of a poem in the first place?
Can you be sure this isn't merely prose chopped
up into linear pieces designed to impersonate a poem?
Is the poet's insistence on colloquial speech really
such a good idea? Does the use of *dodgy* (line 4)
make even the least bit of sense in this context?
If this is free verse, of what in particular is it free?
Is it too late to hope for a rhyme scheme, or maybe
a rhythm that isn't so raggedly haphazard?
How about one measly symbol? A memorable image?
Can you remember any other poems you've read
that might be comparable to this one? And how fair
is that to whatever poem you've just thought of?
Don't you agree that generally poems should avoid
asking questions, that they do nothing but show off
(a) some gratuitous rhetorical effect or (b) the smugness
of the poet, who already knows the answer, or
(c) the poet's own terminally hopeless confusion?

Should it come as any surprise that poetry has such
a limited audience? Are you ready to admit
you made a mistake, and now you'd like to pick
an altogether different poem to respond to?
Will you make your choice judiciously, so as to insure
that in whatever future we might have together,
neither one of us ends up wasting this kind of time?

## Post-Reading Q&A; or, When Van Morrison Finishes a Concert, He's Not Obliged to Do This Sort of Thing

*When did you know you wanted to be a poet?*
I still don't know, but ask me again tomorrow.
It could happen at any moment.

*Would you say your poems depict aspects of your personal philosophy?*
I would never say that.

*What's your primary source of inspiration?*
People who call into late-night-radio talk shows.
I love how they know what they know, how they're so sure
of themselves and so many other amazing things.

*Who are your biggest influences?*
Boss Tweed, Mayor McCheese, and *The Little Taxi That Hurried*.

*Were you born funny?*
No. I was born in the usual manner.

*Do you ever worry that your poems aren't serious enough?*
Thanks a lot—now I'll always worry they aren't serious enough for *you*.

*Shouldn't poetry be socially and politically significant?*
If it's not just a lot of earnest talk and heavy breathing—sure.
But there's also something to be said for the poem-as-Bourbon-Street-reveler.

*Why don't many of your poems rhyme?*
They probably should, but that takes more time.

*How come you don't know more of your poems by heart?*
My heart has room for only so much.
And neither Keats nor Whitman seems in any real hurry to leave.

*There appear to be so many poets these days. Why is that?*
No application. No job interview. And certainly
no pesky job-performance evaluations.
There's always a surplus of poets, yet always a shortage of poetry.

*So you're saying it's hard to write poetry?*
For too many people, apparently, it isn't hard enough.

*How long does it typically take you to write a poem?*
My whole life, more or less, right up until that last line.
Or a couple of hours. Depending.

*Would you be willing to look at my manuscript of poems when this is over?*
And just when I was really hoping this would soon be over.

*Hey, isn't this whole Q&A itself almost like a poem?*
Let's not flatter ourselves. Generally, I do my best work alone.

*Is your conspiratorial Uncle Bud a real person?*
On his best days, yes.

*This Debbie Fuller who shows up in so many of your poems—*
*does she perhaps symbolize love that's always just out of reach?*
Perhaps not. We had a grade-school thing for each other.
She was never more than a desk or two away until her family moved
out of town. But she's still right there whenever I need her.

*Did you really work as a weight-guesser in a seaside carnival?*
Are you absolutely sure you'd like an exact answer, madam?

*Does your poetry have a message and, if so, what is it?*
Yes. Usually it's *Drop what you're doing, meet me on the corner,*
*and bring a lot of money.*

*What's your idea of a great poetry reading?*
Quiet room, big easy chair, sixty watts of soft light, and a poet
whose book is calling for nothing less than my undivided attention.
*That's not quite what I meant.*
I didn't think so, but I quite sincerely wish it was.

*Can reading poetry make you a better person?*
Maybe—but only if you were headed in that general direction anyway.

*Thematically speaking, why—*
Please don't. Anyone speaking thematically is bound to be up to no good.

*Why are you getting steadily more testy?*
Probably because I can't help thinking about Van Morrison, how Van Morrison
 doesn't do things like this, and he's not expected to—he just sings his stocky heart
 out, beautifully, and he's done. He doesn't hang around answering questions about
 songwriting in general, much less his own songs in particular. And Van Morrison's
 not then further expected to come down from the stage and mingle politely, even
 civilly, with his audience, nibbling different-colored cheese cubes and crackers and
 swilling a cup of the mystery punch. Anyway, Van Morrison doesn't have that kind
 of polite *in* him.
Imagine Van Morrison suffering through questions like what exactly constitutes a
 marvelous night for a moondance? What's the deal with Madame George? How
 can a single week, let alone a multiplicity of weeks, be *astral*? In *Tupelo Honey*, did
 he mean to conjure up Tupelo, Mississippi, or some other Tupelo? And was Janet
 Planet really his real girlfriend's name?
And now some kid plants himself right in front of Van Morrison and says *It's so great
 to meet you, man! I've always loved* Brown-Eyed Girl. *I write songs about girls, too.
 I even brought a few of them with me. Could you look at them real quick, tell me
 what you think?* And Van Morrison's still got enough Belfast working-class in him
 to surely lay out this kid cold in no time, but he knows that wouldn't be altogether
 prudent, so instead he tries just walking away with his cheese cubes, but the kid's
 not about to give up now and says *Okay, I could e-mail them to you, then, if you*

*give me your address,* and a woman's trailing both of them, hoping Van Morrison finally sets down his tiny paper plate of cheese cubes so she can surreptitiously pilfer one and later tell her friends that she ate some of Van Morrison's cheese.

But no, Van Morrison will never find himself in that situation. People come to hear him sing. He sings, and then everyone goes home. It's a terrific arrangement, really—so much more than ample pleasure for one night.

*Now why is Van Morrison getting so testy? Who is Van Morrison, anyway, and just who does Van Morrison think he is?*

Van Morrison's not getting testy. In our context here, he's strictly hypothetical. And probably Van Morrison's never once, at least since his teenage skiffle-band days, had to try not sounding ungrateful or impatient when he's asking after the check that's due him because if he doesn't bring it up, it's possible it doesn't *come* up, and even though the host has known about this engagement for months, he'll say something like *You know how Accounts Payable offices are, but you should have it sometime in the next thirty days,* and now that's one more thing I'll no doubt lose track of. But that's just me. Van Morrison never has to keep track of such things because he's a professional, and the concert promoter's a professional, and what's more professional than payment when services are rendered,

so maybe I'm supposed to think that the obligatory dinner will tide me over—where I'm the excuse for a few of the usual English Department suspects to get out of their houses for a free meal at some expensive-but-not-really-worth-it restaurant where they'll load up on appetizers before their pricey entrees and get half-bombed because they're academics and really aren't sure if they should, or even know how to, get all-the-way-bombed, and Van Morrison, were he there, which he isn't and won't be, ever, Van Morrison who knows and loves his Keats and his Yeats and especially his Blake, would be pissed off or just plain too heartsick to eat. He'd bolt for the door before his famously short fuse led to the whole place blowing sky-high.

Van Morrison shows up. Van Morrison sings and goes home.
And no one's ever felt cheated, I promise,
as if this time or any other they didn't get their money's worth.

Hey, with any luck, you folks have come out *ahead*. I know
exactly how much you paid to get in. But right now every one of us
needs to get the hell out of here while we still can, before someone
tries insisting again that what we've just been through,
thematically speaking or otherwise, is any sort of poem at all.

# ⚬ WISCONSIN POETRY SERIES ⚬

Ronald Wallace, Series Editor

(B) = Winner of the Brittingham Prize in Poetry
(FP) = Winner of the Felix Pollak Prize in Poetry
(4L) = Winner of the Four Lakes Prize in Poetry